THE LUCENT LIBRARY OF SCIENCE AND TECHNOLOGY

Energy
Alternatives

by Gabriel Cruden

LUCENT BOOKS

An imprint of Thomson Gale, a part of The Thomson Corporation

Detroit • New York • San Francisco • San Diego • New Haven, Conn. • Waterville, Maine • London • Munich

To Gretchen, who truly made this book possible.

© 2005 Thomson Gale, a part of The Thomson Corporation.

Thomson and Star Logo are trademarks and Gale and Lucent Books are registered trademarks used herein under license.

For more information, contact
Lucent Books
27500 Drake Rd.
Farmington Hills, MI 48331-3535
Or you can visit our Internet site at http://www.gale.com

LIBRARY OF CONGRESS CATALOGING-IN-PUBLICATION DATA

Cruden, Gabriel.
  Energy alternatives / by Gabriel Cruden.
    p. cm. — (The Lucent library of science and technology)
  Includes bibliographical references and index.
  ISBN 1–59018–530–7 (hard cover : alk. paper)
  1. Power resources—Juvenile literature. 2. Renewable energy sources—Juvenile
literature. I. Title. II. Series.
  TJ163.23.C78 2004
  333.79—dc22
                                                              2004010759

Printed in the United States of America

Table of Contents

Foreword

"The world has changed far more in the past 100 years than in any other century in history. The reason is not political or economic, but technological—technologies that flowed directly from advances in basic science."

— Stephen Hawking, "A Brief History of Relativity," *Time*, 2000

The twentieth-century scientific and technological revolution that British physicist Stephen Hawking describes in the above quote has transformed virtually every aspect of human life at an unprecedented pace. Inventions unimaginable a century ago have not only become commonplace but are now considered necessities of daily life. As science historian James Burke writes, "We live surrounded by objects and systems that we take for granted, but which profoundly affect the way we behave, think, work, play, and in general conduct our lives."

For example, in just one hundred years, transportation systems have dramatically changed. In 1900 the first gasoline-powered motorcar had just been introduced, and only 144 miles of U.S. roads were hard-surfaced. Horse-drawn trolleys still filled the streets of American cities. The airplane had yet to be invented. Today 217 million vehicles speed along 4 million miles of U.S. roads. Humans have flown to the moon and commercial aircraft are capable of transporting passengers across the Atlantic Ocean in less than three hours.

The transformation of communications has been just as dramatic. In 1900 most Americans lived and worked on farms without electricity or mail delivery. Few people had ever heard a radio or spoken on a telephone. A hundred years later, 98 percent of American homes have telephones and televisions and more than 50 percent have personal computers. Some families even have more than one television and computer, and cell phones are now commonplace, even among the young. Data beamed from communication satellites routinely predict global weather conditions and fiber-optic cable, e-mail, and the Internet have made worldwide telecommunication instantaneous.

Perhaps the most striking measure of scientific and technological change can be seen in medicine and public health. At the beginning of the twentieth century, the average American life span was forty-seven years. By the end of the century the average life span was approaching eighty years, thanks to advances in medicine including the development of vaccines and antibiotics, the discovery of powerful diagnostic tools such as X rays, the life-saving technology of cardiac and neonatal care, and improvements in nutrition and the control of infectious disease.

Rapid change is likely to continue throughout the twenty-first century as science reveals more about physical and biological processes such as global warming, viral replication, and electrical conductivity, and as people apply that new knowledge to personal decisions and government policy. Already, for example, an international treaty calls for immediate reductions in industrial and automobile emissions in response to studies that show a potentially dangerous rise in global temperatures is caused by human activity. Taking an active role in determining the direction of future changes depends on education; people must understand the possible uses of scientific research and the effects of the technology that surrounds them.

The Lucent Books Library of Science and Technology profiles key innovations and discoveries that have transformed the modern world. Each title strives to make a complex scientific discovery, technology, or phenomenon understandable and relevant to the reader. Because scientific discovery is rarely straightforward, each title

explains the dead ends, fortunate accidents, and basic scientific methods by which the research into the subject
proceeded. And every book examines the practical appli-
cations of an invention, branch of science, or scientific
principle in industry, public health, and personal life, as
well as potential future uses and effects based on ongoing
research. Fully documented quotations, annotated bib-
liographies that include both print and electronic sources,
glossaries, indexes, and technical illustrations are among
the supplemental features designed to point researchers
to further exploration of the subject.

Introduction

New Energy Sources

All living systems require energy to survive. A person requires energy in the form of food. A plant requires energy in the form of sunlight. All mechanical systems also require energy to function. A car needs gasoline to run. A sailboat needs wind to move across the water. Energy, in one form or another, is needed for all living and nonliving activity on the planet. Energy does not actually exist as a thing itself, however. Instead, energy is an idea describing various sources of power.

Long ago, humans relied upon the natural systems of the earth to meet their energy needs. Cliff dwellers of the Southwest built their homes to capture the heat of winter sunlight. Ancient Greeks bathed in water warmed by geothermal vents. Humans around the world used wood to cook their meals and warm their homes. The natural systems of the planet met all of these needs.

The pursuit of more powerful and consistent energy sources came about during the Industrial Revolution, which began in the late eighteenth century and continued through the beginning of the nineteenth century. For the first time, humans began burning fossil fuels in great quantities to meet their energy needs. Fossil fuels powered the factories they worked in, the farm equipment needed to produce large crops, and eventually, the cars they drove. It seemed as if fossil fuels were the perfect answer to the need for a quick and efficient form of energy.

It was not until the 1970s that serious problems from the use of fossil fuels began to be recognized. Oil-producing countries began to demand more money for their product. Oil-consuming countries, such as the United States, refused to accept these higher costs. Many countries put oil embargoes into place. This drove the cost of fossil fuels higher and higher. This series of events led to an energy crisis. People began to wonder what they would do if the cost of fossil fuels did not decline and, consequently, an interest in alternative energy sources began to develop.

Also, since the energy crisis of the 1970s, scientists have learned more about the environmental impact of fossil fuels. They have linked acid rain to the sulfur dioxide released when fossil fuels are burned. Burning fossil fuels also releases large quantities of carbon dioxide. Scientists have found a connection between the growing amount of carbon dioxide in the atmosphere and an increase in global temperatures, referred to as global warming. These discoveries about the effects of fossil fuels have also led to an increased interest in the development of alternative energy sources.

Currently, there are four main alternative energy sources being developed and used today: solar power, wind power, hydropower, and geothermal power. These energy sources, called renewable energy, are all powered by the natural systems of the earth. Unlike fossil fuels, they are also continuously replenished by the earth's natural systems regardless of whether or not they are used. Sunlight will stream down on the planet every day, whether it is captured with solar panels or not. Wind will blow across the land, regardless of turning the rotor of a windmill. Rivers will flow down mountains and geothermal vents will release energy, whether or not their energy is harnessed.

As the resources of the planet are used faster than they are replaced, people are turning to solar, wind, hydro,

and geothermal energy to meet their energy needs. Supporting the use of energy sources that are replenished as fast, or faster, than they are used is helping to create a sustainable energy future. For such changes to happen effectively, however, it will take changes in government policies, more economic support for alternative energy producers, and individual consumers demanding a different choice. These factors will determine the direction of energy production in the coming decades.

Rows of oil derricks crowd the Los Angeles skyline. Humans have been dependent on fossil fuels such as oil as a source of energy for hundreds of years.

Chapter 1

The Development of Energy

Throughout recorded history, humans have searched for ways of putting energy to work for them. Humans have found ways of growing food instead of foraging for it out in the wild. Instead of walking, they ride in cars they have built for getting from one place to another. Humans even learned how to send messages electronically instead of using a messenger or a postal service. This quest for faster, easier, and more efficient ways of meeting the needs of a growing human population has led to increasingly high energy demands. But the resources currently used for generating energy are running out. The pollution created by the use of these resources is also causing significant damage to the planet's natural systems. For these reasons, people are beginning to turn to alternative energy sources to reduce pollution while meeting their energy needs.

A Brief History of Power Use

The sun is by far the oldest source of energy. It has provided heat and light for millions of years and is directly responsible for sustaining all life on earth. Energy, in almost all its forms, starts with the sun. For example, wind is created by temperature changes caused by the sun. Plants and trees, which provide energy in numerous ways, gain their nourishment from the sun. Streams and rivers, providing energy by the force of their downhill flow, are formed from rain and snow. Rain and snow fall at high elevations after being evaporated from lakes and oceans by the sun. The variety of life-forms depending on the sun's energy in one manner or another is impressive.

Although the sun provides vast quantities of energy in many forms, humans could not control it, and so they began to explore other sources of energy. For example, humans discovered a way to generate their own energy from wood, somewhere between five hundred thousand and seven hundred thousand years ago, by most scientists' estimates. At first, wood was burned for warmth, light, and for preparing food. Then the heat from fire began to be used to change the form of some materials to make them more useful, such as clay into pots or bricks, and certain types of metal, such as copper, bronze, and iron, into tools.

This ancient Egyptian mural depicts farmers at work. By exploring new ways to utilize the sun's energy humans began to grow and harvest food.

As the human population increased over time, so did humanity's dependence on fire. This increase in population led to severe shortages of wood in some areas of the world. By the sixteenth century, for instance, Great Britain had so few trees left because of overcutting that the British people had to switch to a completely new source of fuel. In place of trees, they began to use coal. Coal, oil, and gas are called fossil fuels because they are extracted from fossilized plant and animal material from deep under the ground.

Although coal had been used in different parts of the world since the second millennium B.C., its potential uses had not been fully explored. Once coal began to replace wood as a fuel, inventors found many ways that coal could be used as a source of energy. This time of exploration and invention started a period in history called the Industrial Revolution.

The Industrial Revolution marked a big change for people of the world. Many of the agricultural societies that used human muscle power and animals to do work quickly became industrialized and began using machines to do work. When the coal-burning steam engine was invented, a race was begun to see who could create and build bigger, better, and faster machines. The machines were used to provide transportation and to do the work formerly done by people and animals. Coal continued to be used in great quantities until the twentieth century. Then came the invention of the internal combustion engine and the automobile, which used oil and gas instead of coal. Over the years automobiles were modified to use oil and gas more efficiently and with less pollution, but the sheer numbers of automobiles that have come into use over the years have offset the potentially positive impact of these changes. Oil and gas also came into use in other areas, such as for manufacturing and power production, and remain in high use today.

Fossil Fuels

Ever since the Industrial Revolution, humans have sought to generate power from a variety of energy sources. This

remains true today, especially as some energy sources are being used up. Current power needs are continuing to climb while the resources of the planet are steadily being depleted. Technology that operates on electricity, including everything from the typical refrigerator in the kitchen to street lights, is now a part of the lives of most people in industrialized nations, such as the United States. Much of that electricity is generated in power plants, which use large quantities of fossil fuels.

With the advent of the internal combustion engine, machines began to employ oil and gas as fuel. Here, Henry Ford sits on a gas-powered tractor he invented.

The process that created fossil fuels is a natural process of the earth's systems. The remains of plants and animals that died millions of years ago were slowly buried under sediment from the earth and compressed by the weight of the sediment. Over the course of millions of years, the pressure of being compressed by the sediment turned the dead plants and animals into oil, coal, and natural gas. The earth took 500 million years to produce these fuels. Humans have severely depleted them in just over one hundred years, a rate that is 50 million times greater than the rate at which they are formed.

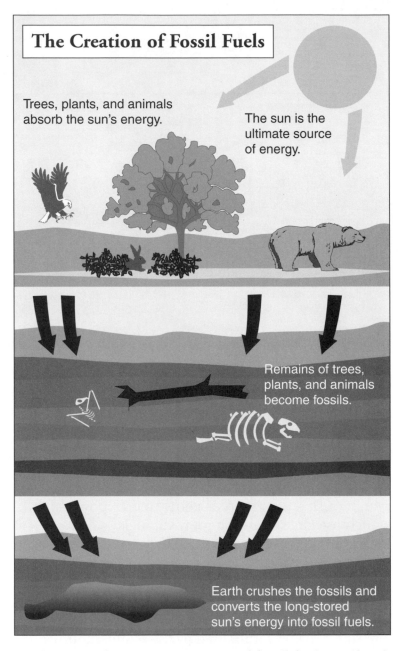

The Creation of Fossil Fuels

Trees, plants, and animals absorb the sun's energy.

The sun is the ultimate source of energy.

Remains of trees, plants, and animals become fossils.

Earth crushes the fossils and converts the long-stored sun's energy into fossil fuels.

There are three primary types of fossil fuels: coal, oil, and natural gas. Coal is a hard, black substance found close to the earth's surface or mined from deep in the ground. There are over two thousand mines in the United States from which more than eight hundred thousand tons of coal are removed each year, supplying approximately 1,566 coal-burning electric power plants. Coal is responsible for providing much of the energy for producing electricity. In fact, there are currently ninety-four new coal-burning power plants that have been proposed, which would power approximately 62 million homes.

Oil can almost be considered a liquid version of coal. It is usually black, but it can also be dark green or even almost clear. Oil is often found underground in dome-shaped spaces directly above coal deposits. Different types of fuels, also called petroleum products, are made from oil, which come in varying thicknesses. Dissolved gases make up the thinnest oils while asphalt oil is regarded as the thickest. Petroleum ether, gasoline, kerosene, gas oil, lubricating oils, and fuel oils are the various grades that fall in between. Much of the oil extracted each year is used in the engines of the various modes of transportation such as cars, trains, boats, and planes. According to a report released by the U.S. Department of Energy, Americans used approximately 19,593,000 barrels of petroleum products a day in 2001.

Natural gas is made up mostly of methane and is highly flammable. Natural gas is thought to have been created from large amounts of plant material that did not become coal. Natural gas will usually flow from a drilled well under its own pressure. In the United States, about 20 trillion cubic feet of gas are produced each year. Natural gas is used primarily for heating purposes and for powering industrial production, especially in manufacturing. According to the U.S. Department of Energy's 1998 Manufacturing Energy Consumption Survey, just six manufacturing industries account for 84 percent of natural gas use, which is primarily for producing heat and steam for making glass, aluminum, metals, wood products, chemicals, and petroleum products. Altogether these fossil fuels are used for about 82 percent of the power produced in the United States.

Nuclear Energy

While fossil fuels are the main source of energy, another of today's energy sources is nuclear power. The first full-scale nuclear power plant in the United States became operational in Shippington, Pennsylvania, in 1957. Nuclear power plants use the energy found in the nuclei of atoms to make electricity. Atoms, which are made of protons, neutrons, and electrons, require a lot of energy to hold these particles together. This energy is released in the form of heat when an atom is split apart. The process of splitting atoms apart is called nuclear fission.

Nuclear power plants harness the heat energy released when nuclear fission occurs. The heat is used to boil water and create steam. The steam is used to turn turbines connected to a generator. As the turbines spin, the generator produces electricity.

A major drawback to nuclear power plants is that they rely upon unstable atoms such as uranium 235 to generate electricity. Unstable atoms are used because they are the easiest to break apart. After uranium 235 undergoes nuclear fission, however, it becomes a highly radioactive waste material that is extremely difficult to dispose of safely.

When nuclear power became a usable source of energy for producing electricity in the 1950s it was thought that it would be the new power for the future. Some sources report that by 1993 about 20 percent of the nation's electricity was generated from nuclear power. Although over one hundred nuclear power plants are still in operation in the United States today, nuclear power has not lived up to its promise. Due to the threat of nuclear accidents and the difficulty and costs associated with the disposal of the toxic waste by-products, nuclear power has not become the primary source of power production it was once thought it would become. Only about 7 to 8 percent of the energy produced in the United States comes from nuclear power.

The Environmental Impact of Modern Power Consumption

Weighing the benefits and drawbacks of one power source versus another is a complicated process. There are many factors to consider, including everything from un-

derstanding the environmental effects of a particular type of power production and consumption, to addressing the power needs of the people and finding methods for delivering the power. Throughout this process, decision makers rely upon scientists to supply the necessary data to make informed decisions. What forms the basis of this science includes the knowledge that carbon dioxide, which is released into the atmosphere when fossil fuels are burned, is creating a lot of harm to the planet and its systems.

Gases that form the atmosphere completely surround the planet. A part of the atmosphere called the ozone layer acts as a sort of shield from the sun, filtering out harmful radiations. Today, human activities release about 433,000 metric tons of nitrous oxide into the atmosphere each year. Nearly 40 percent of the world's nitrous oxide emissions come from burning fossil fuels. The atmosphere has a certain amount of nitrous oxide naturally, but too much nitrous oxide causes a depletion of the ozone layer. Over the last decade scientists have reported that the hole in the ozone layer is growing rapidly.

Giant cooling towers dominate the landscape near a nuclear power plant. Although nuclear fission is an efficient energy source, it produces radioactive waste.

Carbon dioxide is another harmful gas released into the atmosphere. It comes back to the surface as acid rain, poisoning water supplies, killing plants and animals, and eroding and blackening buildings. In addition, carbon dioxide reflects light and heat back to the planet's surface. As the carbon dioxide levels increase in the atmosphere, more heat from the sun is held in, changing the climate of the entire planet by making it warmer. This is called the greenhouse effect and is considered a form of pollution. Author Laughton Johnston claims that, "Carbon dioxide levels in the atmosphere are at their highest in 20 million years."[1]

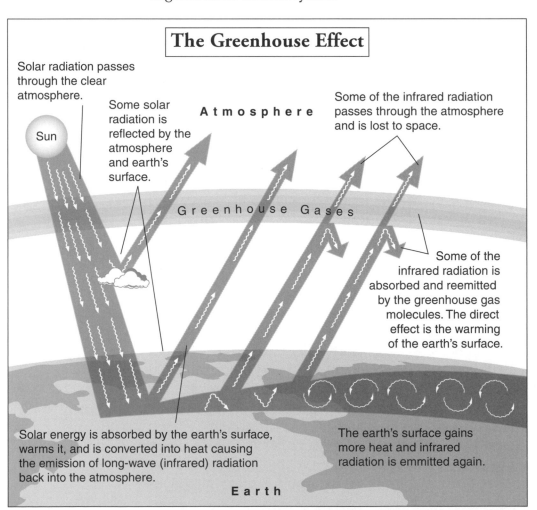

The Greenhouse Effect

Solar radiation passes through the clear atmosphere.

Sun

Some solar radiation is reflected by the atmosphere and earth's surface.

Atmosphere

Some of the infrared radiation passes through the atmosphere and is lost to space.

Greenhouse Gases

Some of the infrared radiation is absorbed and reemitted by the greenhouse gas molecules. The direct effect is the warming of the earth's surface.

Solar energy is absorbed by the earth's surface, warms it, and is converted into heat causing the emission of long-wave (infrared) radiation back into the atmosphere.

The earth's surface gains more heat and infrared radiation is emmitted again.

Earth

The planet Earth operates on delicate systems of natural balance. Scientists believe warming the atmosphere by even a few degrees could cause enormous changes to the environment. Some scientists also believe an increase in the temperature of the planet, brought on by the greenhouse effect, will lead to more weather-related natural disasters such as tornadoes, floods, droughts, and hurricanes. Scientists also predict a significant rise in sea levels, which will reduce land size. Considering that half of the human population lives near a coastline, the effects could be dramatic. In the future, many nations may need to struggle with the question of where all of their people should live if their towns and cities become submerged under oceanic water.

For example, according to a report released by the British Broadcasting Corporation in 2003, the Arctic ice cover is shrinking by an area the size of the Netherlands every year. The Arctic ice cap has thinned from an average thickness of more than nine feet to less than six feet in the last thirty years. In 2002, for the first time in recorded history, a twelve-thousand-year-old ice shelf the size of Luxembourg came adrift from the Antarctic and melted into pieces in just thirty-five days. The glaciers of Kilimanjaro, a mountain in Africa, and of the tropical Andes mountains in South America are melting so fast that experts believe they could disappear within the next twenty years. In October 2001 about eleven thousand people in Tuvalu, a group of nine islands in the Pacific Ocean, tried to abandon their homes because of the rising ocean. The Australian government refused to let them into Australia and so most of the people have remained on the islands, living in fear of being submerged in the ocean.

Burning fossil fuels for energy releases much of the harmful gases that exist today. Scientists estimate that about 35 percent of the greenhouse gases, such as carbon dioxide, being released into the atmosphere are from the United States. With only about 5 percent of the world's population, the United States consumes about one quarter of the world's energy production. At this rate, according to writer Ralph Nansen, "we will destroy both the breathable air and the energy reserves of our only home."[2] In fact, according to a recent BBC Radio Scotland report on global climate change, if the rest of the world consumed energy at the same rate as the United States, "we would need at least two more planet earth's to sustain us all."[3]

Fossil Fuel Supplies Depleted

Not only are these high levels of consumption causing equally high levels of pollution, but the world's fossil fuel supplies are quickly being used up. For example, today's total oil supply is estimated at between 2,000 and 2,800 billion barrels. About 900 billion barrels of oil have already been consumed, 28 million barrels of that just in the year 2000. Addressing resource depletion is not an easy task. As Tom Hansen, vice president of Tucson Electric Power, says, "It is like trying to change the wings of an airplane while you are in flight." He describes a difficult process, but one with what he considers a great payoff. "We have to wean ourselves off traditional fuels, because it is going to get harder for us to build more power plants and install more transmission lines."[4]

The future of energy production will certainly determine what the overall health of the planet will be. Most scientists agree that the choices that support fossil fuel use will only worsen the environmental damage that has already occurred. Instead, choosing to look to renewable energy sources and energy conservation techniques offers the potential to improve the health of the planet. This belief concerning the future of renewable energy is voiced by author Melvin A. Benarde in his book, *Our Precarious Habitat*. "There are no instant cures, no ready-made solutions," Benarde writes. "This does not mean there is no hope for a future. On the contrary, there is a great deal; but it will take time and money — lots of money—and a willingness on the part of the people to see it through."[5]

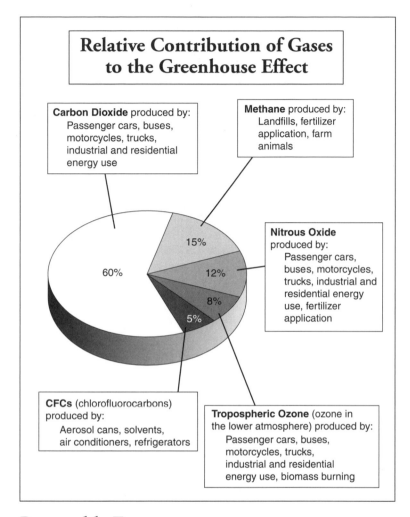

Relative Contribution of Gases to the Greenhouse Effect

Carbon Dioxide produced by: Passenger cars, buses, motorcycles, trucks, industrial and residential energy use

Methane produced by: Landfills, fertilizer application, farm animals

Nitrous Oxide produced by: Passenger cars, buses, motorcycles, trucks, industrial and residential energy use, fertilizer application

60%

15%

12%

8%

5%

CFCs (chlorofluorocarbons) produced by: Aerosol cans, solvents, air conditioners, refrigerators

Tropospheric Ozone (ozone in the lower atmosphere) produced by: Passenger cars, buses, motorcycles, trucks, industrial and residential energy use, biomass burning

Renewable Energy

Because energy is usable power, the form that the energy is in can be used up. When a combustion engine car runs out of gasoline, it loses its power and can no longer operate until more fuel is put into the system. If a power plant that generates electricity by burning coal runs out of coal, then it can no longer generate electricity until more coal is put into the power plant burners.

Renewable energy, on the other hand, is energy that is replaced at the same rate that it is used. Renewable energy is replaced through natural processes or through sound management practices, and so it is a source of power that does not run out. A perfect example of renewable energy is energy from the sun, which comes in an abundant supply every day.

Other examples of renewable sources of energy include the wind, the waves and tides, the gravitational pull of the earth, the heat at the earth's core (geothermal energy), landfill gases, and, to a limited degree, trees and plant material. Many of these renewable sources of energy can be used in their raw form. They are natural forces that create energy without the help of humans. All that is needed is for someone to decide how that energy can be used. Building a sail for a boat makes use of the wind. Building a waterwheel on a river makes use of the flowing water that is pulled downhill by the earth's gravity. Building a house out of glass—a greenhouse—traps the heat from sunlight inside, providing warmth and allowing plants to grow where they might not otherwise grow.

The Case for Renewable Energy

Renewable energy, also called "green energy," or "clean energy," does not deplete natural resources and creates little-to-no pollution when it is generated. Throughout history, renewable sources of energy have been used by various peoples to supply power for their specific needs, but always on a small scale. The unique challenge of today is finding a way to supply renewable energy to entire populations. Large-scale energy production requires specialized equipment such as energy storage and transmission facilities. The technology for generating the power must also be efficient and cost-effective to produce and operate.

In the face of big-oil-company interests and the politics of government, it has taken a long time for renewable energy options to even be considered on a large scale. The scientific and technological development of solar power, for example, looked promising when in 1977 President Jimmy Carter initiated a plan to develop solar energy and other alternative fuels. His goal for the nation was to have 20 percent of its power coming from solar power generation by the year 2000, and he started by putting solar panels on the White House. By the late 1970s, however, big oil companies had bought up most of the patents for the solar technologies being developed. The Reagan administration took the solar panels off of the White House and spent billions of dollars on the military, foreign aid, and for research and production of atomic weapons instead of on renewable energy.

Since that time, government support for the research and development of renewable energy has not been easy to get, and the technology has been slow to come into its own. Despite these setbacks, independent companies are now making renewable energy products that, while still costly to purchase, offer cheap, clean, renewable energy to the consumer. In his book *Charging Ahead,* writer,

In 1977 President Jimmy Carter speaks about the importance of alternative energy sources during a dedication of a solar heating system installed on the White House.

teacher, and environmental science and policy consultant John J. Berger says of renewable energy sources that "modern science and engineering technology have of late made them much more efficient, convenient, and economical."[6] Steve Kretzmann, coordinator for the Greenpeace Global Warming Campaign, shares a similar point of view: "One of the greatest myths surrounding clean energy is that it is not ready to do the job. Renewables *are* ready—the technical barriers are almost entirely removed. The true barriers to energy reform are now, and always have been, political."[7]

Many experts agree that renewable energy would provide numerous benefits. Berger, for example, says that:

> Because renewables do not use fossil fuels (most are entirely fuel-free) they are largely immune to the threat of future oil or gas shortages and fossil fuel price hikes. For the same reason, because most renewable technologies require no combustion, they are far kinder to the environment than coal, oil, and natural gas. Smog and acid rain could be eliminated with renewables. The collective lungs of America could breathe a sigh of relief.[8]

In addition to being virtually nonpolluting, renewable energy is thought to be cheaper for producers and consumers. As reported in a book commissioned in 1992 by the United Nations Solar Energy Group on Environment and Development, "Given adequate support, renewable energy technologies can meet much of the growing demand at prices lower than those usually forecast for conventional energy."[9] As the human population continues to increase and the energy needs of the world climb, renewable energy is seen more and more as the only alternative.

Chapter 2

Solar Power

Sunlight is an energy source that is available to varying degrees every single day. Sunlight has been used in various ways since the beginning of human history. Today, advanced technologies are used to deliver the power generated from sunlight through small-scale solar power collection sites, as well as through power-generating plants that serve large populations. Solar power technology is still developing and has also met with strong resistance by the government and large oil companies. Despite these obstacles this technology holds great potential for generating nonpolluting energy for the world.

Passive Heating

Humans have attempted to use solar power for their own benefit throughout history. Native Americans of the Southwest chose to build their homes into the south-facing sides of cliffs to capture the sun's warmth. They observed that the sun was in the southern sky during the coldest months of the year and positioned their dwellings to trap the heat from the sun. The Romans took a similar approach, only they also developed and installed glass in their windows, which allowed light in but kept heat from escaping.

Using the sun's energy in this way is called passive heating and is only one of the many ways solar power can be harnessed. It is called passive because there is no expenditure of energy in trapping the power from the sun. This technique is still applied today. Like the cliff

The sun is the ultimate source of all of the energy on earth. Throughout history, humans have attempted to harness solar power for their benefit.

dwellers of the Southwest, people living in a community called Esperanza del Sol (Hope for the Sun) in Dallas, Texas, are using these same techniques. All of the people in this community live in homes with large roof overhangs. These overhangs block the hot summer sun and keep the air inside the home cool. The sun travels much lower in the winter and so the sunlight is then able to come through the windows and warm the air inside the home. This simple construction feature allows the people of Esperanza del Sol to feel much more comfortable in their homes regardless of what season it is. In addition, because they are not relying on fossil fuels to create electricity to power an air conditioner or heating system, they pay much less in energy bills and are helping to reduce the damage being done to the environment.

Flat Plate Collectors

Flat plate collectors, a form of passive heating that uses sunlight to heat water, work in much the same way as using sunlight to heat a home. By running water through a glass-topped box, black inside, and installed on the roof of a home, the energy from the sun can be used to heat the water. This technology was used in an informal way during the pioneer days and was later developed into a more formal system in the 1970s.

Flat plate collectors can be built in a variety of ways and range anywhere from about four feet square to the size of the entire roof. A common design includes a series of black tubes, filled with water or antifreeze, that run through the box. The water or antifreeze in these

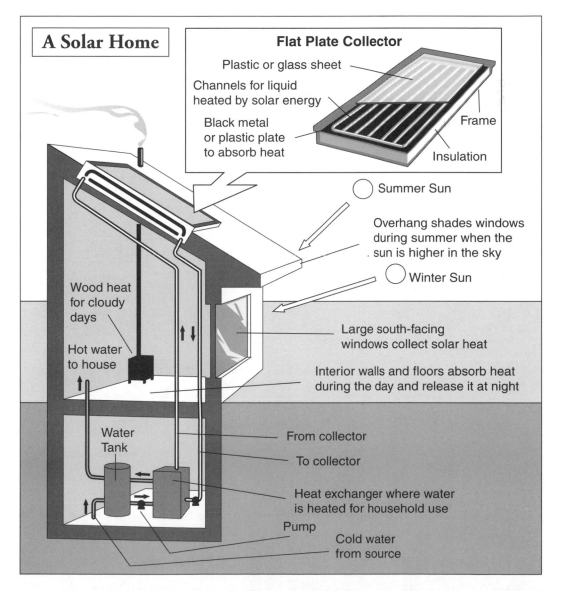

A Solar Home

Flat Plate Collector

Plastic or glass sheet

Channels for liquid heated by solar energy

Black metal or plastic plate to absorb heat

Frame

Insulation

Summer Sun

Overhang shades windows during summer when the sun is higher in the sky

Winter Sun

Wood heat for cloudy days

Hot water to house

Large south-facing windows collect solar heat

Interior walls and floors absorb heat during the day and release it at night

Water Tank

From collector

To collector

Heat exchanger where water is heated for household use

Pump

Cold water from source

tubes can heat up to more than 160 degrees Fahrenheit in less than an hour under direct sunlight. With a flat plate collector that holds water, the homeowner can shower, bathe, wash clothes, or do dishes using the heated water directly from the flat plate collector. If the tubes hold antifreeze, then the heated antifreeze fluid can be pumped through tubes in a water storage tank, heating the water in the tank for use in the home.

Solar Trough Collectors

The photovoltaic panels of this solar energy plant in California's Mojave Desert produce enough electricity to power thousands of homes.

Although there are over eight hundred thousand solar water heaters, such as flat plate collectors, in operation in America today, most of these serve only the needs of individual homes or small businesses. Scientists have been working hard to find ways to make solar heating more applicable to large populations. Solar trough col-

lectors are one solution scientists in the Mojave Desert of California have been examining as a way to serve large numbers of people at once. At this site, nine sets of sixty-four curved mirrors (which are about 2 ½ feet by just over 4 feet) are used to focus sunlight onto tubes that run along the center of the curved mirrors. Synthetic oils in the tubes, which are about 150 feet long, absorb the solar energy and heat up, reaching temperatures around 735 degrees Fahrenheit. Because the fluid inside the tubes is so hot, merely running the tube through a large vat of water causes the water to boil. The steam from the boiling water is then used to drive a turbogenerator, which creates electricity. This site in California is currently generating about a third of the energy production of a large nuclear plant, or enough energy to power 350,000 homes.

The power generated in this fashion is not yet efficient, costing more than twice as much as fossil fuels at about twelve cents per kilowatt. However, scientists are researching how to improve this type of solar energy collection and decrease the cost of the materials.

The Solar Furnace

In the Pyrenees mountains of France is another large-scale experimental solar power system. In the 1970s scientists constructed a solar furnace capable of reaching temperatures so high that it can melt metal. The builders of the furnace chose a location at about five thousand feet up in the mountains to guarantee clear skies for their project.

The solar furnace is much larger than a solar trough, mainly because it uses hundreds of flat mirrors, called heliostats, to collect sunlight over a much larger area. This sunlight is bounced onto a single curved mirror the size of a ten-story building. Since the mirror is curved, the sunlight can be focused onto one central tower opposite it. Like the solar trough collector, this central tower, which looks somewhat like a large water tower, uses the sunlight to create electricity by heating fluids to create steam to run through a turbogenerator.

The solar furnace effectively generates about one thousand kw of energy, enough to power more than six hundred homes. However, it is still used as a research site, as duplicates of the furnace are still too expensive to build and operate competitively.

The Electrical Side of Solar Power

Using sunlight to heat fluids to run turbogenerators is not the only way energy can be harnessed from the sun to create electricity. Sunlight can also be captured in photovoltaic (PV) cells, which make up the common solar panel seen on everything from calculators to rooftops. A PV cell is constructed of a thin, small wafer of silicon that is about two inches square. One side of the wafer is dipped in a boron solution. This is a solution that contains atoms that want to give up electrons. The other side of the wafer is dipped in a phosphorus solution that has atoms that want to take electrons. When sunlight strikes the top side of the wafer, it gives boron atoms a lot of energy. This burst of energy causes the boron atoms to give up their additional electrons. A thin metal wire is attached to both sides of a PV cell. Because metal is composed of atoms that attract electrons, the electrons that were given up by the boron atoms move toward the wire and travel down it in the form of electricity. An appliance or machine plugged into the wire can then use the electricity. When the electricity has run through the appliance or machine, it returns via the wire to the phosphorus side of the PV cell. Eventually these electrons pass through the silicon wafer back to the boron side of the PV cell. These electrons can be used over and over to create electricity. One or two small PV cells are commonly used to power such items as small calculators and watches.

PV Cell Modules

Many of these PV cells must be linked together to create enough electricity to power most electrical motors. For instance, a solar-powered car would need about 375 PV cells to run efficiently. When PV cells are linked together by running a wire from one PV cell to the next, they are called modules. The more cells collecting energy and funneling it to one destination, such as an electric motor, the more power that motor receives. The National Aeronautics and Space Administration (NASA) first used solar modules in 1959 to power the *Vanguard 1* satellite. This was a perfect solution to the power needs of space exploration, as solar modules are lightweight, durable, and require little-to-no maintenance. Sunlight is also in constant abundance in space.

Today, people are finding that solar modules are an excellent option when they do not have immediate access to electricity through conventional power lines. Owners

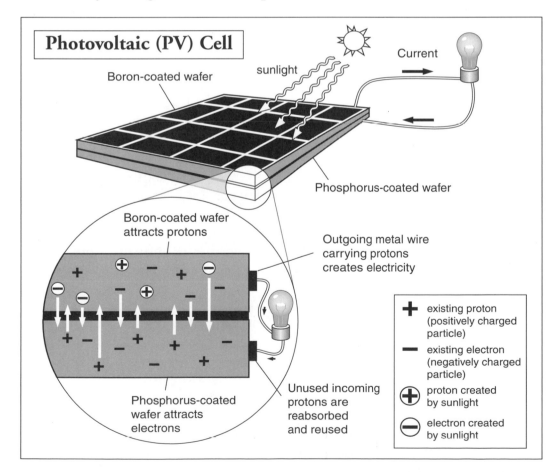

Photovoltaic (PV) Cell

Boron-coated wafer

sunlight

Current

Phosphorus-coated wafer

Boron-coated wafer attracts protons

Outgoing metal wire carrying protons creates electricity

Phosphorus-coated wafer attracts electrons

Unused incoming protons are reabsorbed and reused

+ existing proton (positively charged particle)

− existing electron (negatively charged particle)

⊕ proton created by sunlight

⊖ electron created by sunlight

of recreational vehicles and boats can place solar modules on the roof of an RV or on the deck of a boat to capture energy. This energy can then be used to power small appliances on board, such as stoves, refrigerators, and radios.

More commonly seen, perhaps, is the use of solar modules to power traffic signals, road signs, and streetlights. The signs and road signals are often in remote areas where it would be far too expensive to run electrical lines to the site. Instead, road departments choose to use solar modules to generate electricity from the sun to power the equipment.

For people who live far away from any source of electricity to power their homes or businesses, solar modules are sometimes a solution. These solar modules may be attached to the roof of a home or may be on freestanding bases. In either case, the modules are angled toward the sun to capture the most energy. As the sun's angle to the earth varies throughout the year, the owners often reset the angle of the modules to capture the most energy from the sun. Depending on the size and number of modules, a home can be powered solely by solar modules. For example, the typical homeowner could meet his or her energy needs with an array of eight standard 120-watt PV cell modules. Counts of current solar power usage are difficult to make due to their rural distribution. The most recent count to date was released in a CNN report in late 1997, showing that over ten thousand homes in the United States were entirely powered by solar energy.

Solar-Powered Cars

Scientists are also applying solar energy techniques to cars. Solar-powered cars, first built in Chicago in 1955, may become the wave of the future, but for now they are used mostly for competitions instead of the public market. The main barrier is the price of construction, which can run as much as $80,000 to $120,000. This high cost comes from the fact that the parts and energy collection and storage systems are expensive and not

made on a production-level scale, which would greatly reduce the price.

Another type of solar-powered car being actively developed is actually an electric car that is primarily charged by solar panels while it is parked and runs off of a battery while in use. "The typical car is charged up via an electrical outlet, which could be powered by solar-powered carports and parking garages," explains Jennifer Carless, author of *Renewable Energy: A Concise Guide to Green Alternatives.* "PV panels in the roofs would provide enough energy to charge cars on sunny days, which would be more energy-efficient than refining petroleum."[10]

Another version is the fuel cell car which runs off of hydrogen. Solar energy is used to generate hydrogen at a station where a car can fill up, similar to existing gas stations. The way this works is that solar energy is collected from the sun to generate electricity. The electricity is then applied to water, breaking it into its parts, hydrogen and oxygen. The hydrogen, which is flammable, is used as a combustible gas while the oxygen is released harmlessly into the atmosphere. Hydrogen fuel cells can be used again and again.

This three-wheeled electric car runs on batteries charged by a solar panel in its roof.

Currently, there are hydrogen filling stations in use in Germany and Japan, as well as a display model built by the Ford Motor Company in Dearborn, Michigan, in 1999. Scientists project a massive reduction—about 16.4 percent in the United States—in the use of fossil fuels if solar power technology is applied to the automobile industry.

Sunlight: Free and Nonpolluting

There are many benefits to using solar power. First and foremost, solar power is available wherever the sun shines—which is, for the most part, anywhere on the planet. People living in developing countries are using more and more solar power as they begin to establish cities and towns. Up to 80 percent of the solar modules created in the United States are exported to third world countries. These countries are using solar energy to power everything from village wells to the first solar-powered hospital, as is being done in Mali, Africa.

John Schaeffer, president and founder of Real Goods, states, "There are still 2 billion of the world's 6 billion people who have no electricity. Bringing them electricity from solar instead of fossil fuels makes more sense."[11]

Indeed, if these countries can plan how they want to develop, they may be able to create systems that are entirely self-sustaining through the use of solar power. This would mean that they would not have to rely on other countries for energy. They would also be able to step away from all of the pollution problems industrialized nations now face through the abundant use of fossil fuels.

Economically speaking, solar energy is a wise choice. According to Carless, "The cost of running a PV system reduces to zero after buying and installing it."[12] A solar power system has a high initial investment cost, but once it is paid for there is little-to-no maintenance cost. The savings from not having energy bills to pay will cover the cost in five to ten years. After that, energy is free for the lifetime of the solar modules, which are usually guaranteed for at least twenty-five years. Considering how the cost of electrical bills can add up over time, this is quite an attractive aspect of solar energy. In many cases, using solar energy not only frees people of monthly energy bills, but local power companies will buy the excess power generated by solar power systems if the homes are connected to the utility company through their power lines. Unused electricity can then be of financial benefit to the solar power system owner and can be made available for use by other customers.

Overall, solar power has a lot to offer, as the authors of *The Almanac of Renewable Energy* assert. "PV technology is an inherently clean source of electricity. During power generation, PV arrays produce no noise, acid rain, smog, carbon dioxide, water pollutants, or nuclear wastes."[13]

The Limitations of Solar Power

Although solar power could be seen as the answer to the world's energy needs, it does have some significant drawbacks. Some of these drawbacks are inherent in the use of any energy source. Other drawbacks are unique to solar power.

This house on a small South Pacific island uses solar panels to provide energy. Many people living in developing countries rely on solar power.

It is true that solar power is available for use wherever the sun is shining. One major problem, however, is that the sun only shines during daylight hours. Cloudy days also reduce the effectiveness of solar modules. Unfortunately, the evening hours and cloudy days are the times when energy needs are at their highest. During the evening people are home from work and are busy making dinner, watching television, and taking baths. On a cloudy day people use a lot of energy to heat their homes. This means another source of energy needs to be used in the evening hours or during a particularly cloudy day.

For people currently using solar power, these secondary sources of energy are often generators. Generators cause noise pollution and emit many gases that contribute to the greenhouse effect and global warming. Many of the environmental benefits of solar power are lost when generators are used as a secondary source of power.

Some people circumvent the need for a generator by storing the energy generated by their solar modules during the day in a series of deep cell batteries. These batteries are designed to have a long life of ten to twenty years and to not be damaged by daily recharging. Yet once these batteries have expired, they too become a source of pollution that needs to be carefully disposed of.

Another reason solar power is not widely used is because it often is greatly misunderstood by members of the general public. During the energy crisis of the 1970s many people became interested in alternative energy sources. One of the main sources explored was solar power. At the time, much was still unknown about solar power, and scientists were still discovering the best ways for this energy to be utilized. Yet some solar energy companies attempted to make a quick profit in the budding market, making extreme claims about their products, which were often shoddy and had less than one-tenth the operating power of the modules made today. As these solar panels failed to deliver the energy promised by the companies, many people became dissatisfied with solar power as a whole. This has led to a long-lasting mistrust of solar power. Today, most people do not realize how simple a solar power system is to install and operate and the energy potential it can offer.

A Bright Future

Even though many people know little about solar power technology, the general population is becoming educated about the environmental degradation of the planet and the long-term effects this will have. Many understand why global warming is occurring and what role their energy use choices play in it. International relationships are becoming strained because of a dependence on oil. All of these factors have led to many people wanting better energy alternatives to be available for use. "Interest in PV power remains high and appears to be growing," states the *Almanac of Renewable*

Sunlight glints off of a sea of solar panels near Bakersfield, California. With increasing public concern for the environment, alternatives to fossil fuels, such as solar power, are also on the rise.

Energy. "Policy makers and the public alike have become increasingly concerned about the environmental impacts of fossil fuels and nuclear energy. In addition, the Gulf War, like the energy crises of the 1970s, demonstrated the economic and political costs of the world's heavy dependence on oil." [14]

Scientists are now exploring better methods of collecting and storing solar power. From the 1970s to now, PV cells have become 40 percent more effective in collecting sunlight. This means people using solar power today require roughly half the number of solar modules as they did thirty years ago to create the same amount of electricity. This also means consumers have to spend less to get the same result and need less room for mounting the panels. Due to these changes the future for solar power appears bright, although it will require government, public, and financial backing to become a reality.

Many power companies are also eager to explore other methods for creating electricity so they can more consistently supply power to their customers, avoiding rolling blackouts and sometimes frequent brownouts. Environmentalists, many scientists, and conscientious consumers are holding out for the day when solar power is used consistently by utilities as a standard source of their energy supply. "Then," says author Jennifer Carless, "we will be making practical and widespread use of a free, environmentally benign energy source." [15]

Chapter 3

Wind Power

Throughout history the wind has been used by humans as an energy source for such things as transportation and food production. Energy released by the trade winds—winds that almost always blow in the same direction—was first captured in the sails of ships and used to transport the ship and its cargo across oceans. There are few large ships that still use wind power, although many people continue to enjoy sailing smaller crafts using the power of wind.

Food production, such as grinding flour for baking bread, was sometimes powered by wind-driven windmills. Those windmills were eventually modified to run water pumps and even later, to generate electricity. Today, the modern windmill, called a wind turbine, is used to generate large quantities of electricity. Through advances in technology, energy producers can even generate electricity from a whole series of wind turbines, called a wind farm. These wind farms are beginning to spread through parts of the United States and the rest of the world.

Harnessing the Wind

For centuries farmers have used windmills to harness the wind to grind grain into flour for baking. Windmills were known to be in use in Europe as long ago as the twelfth century. In more recent history, the windmill was adapted for pumping water to irrigate fields, to provide drinking water, or to run small sawmills. This type of windmill was quite common on farms in the United States until the 1940s when utility companies became

Throughout history, sails have been used to harness the power of the wind to propel watercraft like these sailboats.

more widespread and many farmers began to use more modern forms of electricity.

A classic windmill has a fairly simple design with several blades on a rotor that turns on top of a tower as the wind blows through them. Blades may be constructed of various materials, including wood, cloth, and metal. They generally have a large surface to capture as much wind power as possible. The tower they sit atop can also be quite tall, sometimes up to fifty feet, as the wind tends to be stronger higher above the ground.

As the wind blows, it turns the blades of the windmill, which spin a central shaft (or pole) that extends from the top to the bottom of the tower of the windmill. The spinning shaft may be attached to many different mechanisms at the base of the windmill, depending upon the windmill's use. If a farmer wishes to grind grain, the spinning shaft is attached to a gear that turns a grain mill; if the farmer wants to pump water into the fields, the shaft is designed to drive a pump.

Despite the age of this technology, many water-pumping windmills are still used in rural areas of developing countries to irrigate field crops. For example, more than three hundred thousand wind-driven water pumps are in place in parts of South Africa as a low-cost, low-maintenance method of supplying water to people, livestock, and fields. In rural United States, however, few water-pumping windmills are used except in some remote areas such as parts of west Texas, where the water is needed mainly for cattle. There, windmills are used because it is too difficult and expensive to string miles and miles of power lines to those remote areas.

Wind Turbines: The Modern Windmill

Wind turbines work much like windmills, but they are used specifically to generate electricity. A wind turbine usually has fewer blades and is made of lighter materials, such as plastics, which allow the blades to turn more quickly and with less wind. The blades of the wind turbine capture the energy of the wind and send it down a shaft inside the nacelle. This shaft spins the turbines of a generator. Inside the generator is a large pole with metal wires wrapped around it. On the inside walls of the generator are magnets. As the turbine poles spin, the magnets draw electrons from the wire and produce electricity. A wind turbine can produce enough electricity to satisfy the needs of a home. In some cases, a single

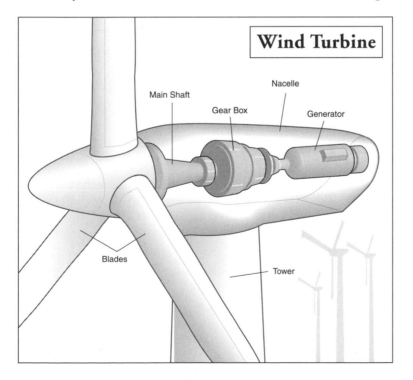

Wind Turbine

Main Shaft
Nacelle
Gear Box
Generator
Blades
Tower

turbine may also produce excess energy that can be stored in batteries or sold to a local utility company.

Wind turbines can also be grouped together to create large quantities of electricity. This is referred to as a wind farm. Wind farms are becoming more widespread throughout the world. In Denmark, for example, 10 percent of its power needs are met with wind farms. Denmark has also created laws that allow wind machine owners to easily sell their excess electricity to local utility companies. Often, individual families in Denmark will buy several large wind machines that produce enough electricity to power the homes of fifty to seventy-five families. Since the Danish government fully supports this form of green energy, the use of wind power is expected to keep increasing in their country. It is estimated that in northern European countries, including Denmark, nearly three times the amount of electricity is produced by wind machines than in the United States. This figure is expected to increase even more as several developing countries, such as Argentina, Pakistan, and a number of African countries, are exploring the use of wind farms as they establish their own energy infrastructures.

In the United States, California, followed by Texas, generates the most electricity from wind farms. California was also the first state to pursue wind farm development in the early 1980s. Wind farms have been slow to develop in the United States, however, due in part to the high cost for building and then maintaining the facilities. Independent ownership, which is how most of the wind farms in the United States are owned, is also more expensive than utility-owned wind farms. But in recent years the towers and rotors of wind turbines have been made much bigger, from 50 feet to 180 feet, producing more energy at a lower cost. In fact, the overall cost of wind power generation has fallen by about 90 percent over the last twenty years.

Plentiful Winds

Like solar power, wind power is a renewable energy source. The energy of the sun drives the production of

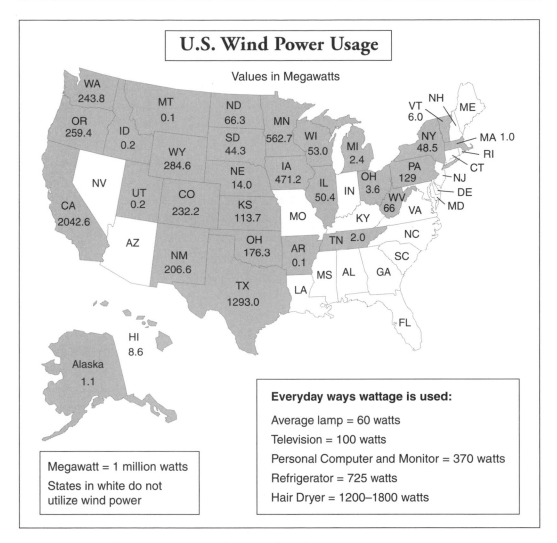

U.S. Wind Power Usage

Values in Megawatts

WA 243.8
OR 259.4
ID 0.2
MT 0.1
ND 66.3
MN 562.7
WI 53.0
MI 2.4
VT 6.0
NH
ME
NY 48.5
MA 1.0
RI
CT
NV
UT 0.2
WY 284.6
SD 44.3
NE 14.0
IA 471.2
IL 50.4
IN
OH 3.6
PA 129
NJ
DE
MD
CA 2042.6
CO 232.2
KS 113.7
MO
KY
WV 66
VA
AZ
NM 206.6
OH 176.3
AR 0.1
TN 2.0
NC
SC
MS
AL
GA
TX 1293.0
LA
FL
HI 8.6
Alaska 1.1

Everyday ways wattage is used:

Average lamp = 60 watts

Television = 100 watts

Personal Computer and Monitor = 370 watts

Refrigerator = 725 watts

Hair Dryer = 1200–1800 watts

Megawatt = 1 million watts

States in white do not utilize wind power

wind. Since the sun is in daily supply, the energy required to create wind is continuously available. Unlike solar power, however, the energy of wind is also present during the nighttime as land and water absorb the heat of the sun.

Wind power can also be available in great supply. Strong and consistent winds tend to occur where there are large areas of flat land, such as prairies and deserts, that are heated by sunlight. The midwestern United States, such as North and South Dakota, Colorado, Kansas, Nebraska, Iowa, Indiana, Illinois, Minnesota, and Ohio, is an ideal place for the creation of such winds. The American Wind Energy Association calculates there is enough available land in the Midwest, or in just one hundred square miles of Nevada's windiest areas, to house enough wind farms to meet the energy needs of the entire United States. The construction of wind farms would do little to alter these landscapes, as farming of crops and wind power generation could occur on the same lands.

Winds are generated in high amounts in desert areas. The desert sands trap the heat of the sun and slowly release the energy throughout the troposphere during the night. One such desert area, Tehachapi-Mojave, California, is home to a wind farm of five thousand wind turbines. This wind farm can produce enough electricity to satisfy the needs of five hundred thousand homes at a cost of four cents per kilowatt-hour. This cost is comparable to the other local energy sources. As the efficiency of wind farms increases, this cost will decrease even further.

Small-Scale Production Potential

Wind power can also be produced on a smaller scale, serving the needs of rural homes. A home that is off the grid (not connected to the utility company) and in a windy location can easily tap into the power of the wind. Such a home simply needs a stand-alone wind machine. The wind machine takes up relatively little space and does not alter the natural landscape. These are two strong arguments for anyone that hopes to have electricity in a remote home, but does not wish to change the natural environment surrounding the home.

Although the initial investment for such small wind systems is quite high, the cost of energy is reduced in the long run. A typical wind system can be installed for twenty thousand dollars and pay for itself within ten years. In addition, a wind turbine requires minimal maintenance, such as keeping the moving parts lubricated. Currently the average cost of producing one kilowatt-hour of electricity using wind power is about six cents, although some wind farms can produce at a lower cost. This is only slightly more than the cost of producing electricity by burning fossil fuels. As the cost of burning fossil fuels to create electricity increases yearly throughout the nation, this feature of wind power becomes more and more attractive.

Some Drawbacks

Wind power can be an easily viable source of energy for many people, but there are some drawbacks. Perhaps the biggest drawback to wind power is that a person must live in a windy area to harness it. These areas tend to be rather flat or desertlike and do not often attract many people. In addition, few people tend to use stand-alone systems in these areas, as more traditional sources of electricity are already available. These areas can still be used to build wind farms, however, as the electricity produced can be connected to the grid.

Even when living in a windy area, the wind cannot be counted on to always be blowing. Some days are windier than others and some seasons are prone to higher winds than others. With such an intermittent source of power, the electricity produced by wind turbines often requires battery storage. These batteries generally have a long life span of about ten to twenty years, but eventually require replacement. As with solar power systems that use batteries to store energy, battery disposal is an issue as the materials used to create batteries are toxic to the environment.

Some people prefer to use gasoline-powered generators as a secondary source of power on the days when there is little wind. These generators usually burn fossil fuels. The burning of fossil fuels contributes to air pollution. It also emits greenhouse gases, which are damaging to the atmosphere.

Wind machines can also cause noise pollution. The whirling of the blades and the spinning of the turbine

In areas where wind power is abundant, wind farms like this one in Palm Springs, California, can generate electricity in a very cost-effective manner.

in a ten-kilowatt wind machine positioned three hundred feet from a home produces noise that is comparable to wind blowing through trees. Many people find this noise to be an irritant and consider it noise pollution.

For some people wind machines are a pleasing sight. The straight lines against a blue sky make a beautiful view. For others wind machines and wind farms are an eyesore. They disrupt the view and break up the natural landscape. The blades are dizzying, the towers block the sun, and their bases are large blocks of unattractive cement.

Deadly to Birds

Wind machines can also have an environmental impact on wildlife. They are considered something of a hazard to migratory birds. The birds fly into the blades and are killed. Since many migratory birds already suffer the hardship of lost habitat, this can pose quite a secondary threat to their population. For example, in a study conducted in 1992 by the California Energy Commission, thirty-nine golden eagles, out of about five hundred breeding pairs, were killed at the Altamont Pass wind farm. For this reason, scientists are studying the flight patterns of migratory birds more thoroughly, and wind farmers are trying not to build in migratory birds' flight paths.

Researchers are also experimenting with painting the blades to make the blades more visible to birds. For example, instead of the usual white, researchers are painting the blades with black and orange stripes. "We go out and look for any environmental issues or concerns, like migratory birds' flight paths, water fowl, any threatened or endangered plants or animals, as well as for any cultural artifacts," says Vito Giarrusso, Florida Power and Light Operations production manager for the Stateline Wind Project. "We have to make sure we aren't in, around, or imposing on any of those."[16]

A Changing Industry

Wind machines are becoming more popular as their reliability increases. Wind machines are also becoming far more simplified in structure and no longer require as much maintenance. In the early days of the industry, blades were made from materials such as wood and cloth that needed frequent repair or replacement, the internal workings of the machines needed regular lubrication, and the overall size of the structures was small compared to those of today. Scientists and technicians are working to improve the efficiency of wind turbines even further, which would provide a boost to the wind power industry. Some of the specifics of the investigations include redesigning the shape of the blades and the materials they are made of, improving the internal mechanisms, and exploring optimum locations for the machines.

The largest wind farm now under construction in the United States is being built by American National Wind Power. The wind farm, located in Texas, is expected to have the capacity to supply sixty thousand homes with electricity. David Butterworth, the head of business development at American National Wind Power, believes this project will be a success. "Texas residents have expressed a preference for energy from clean, renewable sources," he said. "Wind power is one of the cleanest and greenest of all the commercial methods for generating electricity. It produces no gas emissions which contribute to global warming and climate change, no waste products and no radioactive contaminants."[17]

Consumer and Company Support Critical

Many wind farm developers feel that as wind power becomes better understood and accepted by the American consumer, the wind farm industry will become a viable power choice in the U.S. energy market. The 1990s saw a massive increase in the use of stand-alone wind machines in the United States. That trend has continued with about five times as many wind machines now in use as there were in 1995. Today, people living off the grid in appropriately windy locations are building their homes with wind power in mind. Many are now looking at the environmental and economic impacts of their energy choices and are choosing wind power. This consumer demand for wind power will be a critical factor in its development. Wind machine owners may ask to net meter the electricity they produce at their own homes. This means they can generate electricity using wind power and sell their excess electricity to the power company. Sonja Ling of the Renewable Northwest Project believes, "Net-metering for small-scale, clean, renewable energy systems is one important step towards diversifying the region's energy mix and reducing our over-dependence on hydropower and fossil fuels."[18] In other words, every small contribution to the net amount of electricity will serve to make a difference in the long term.

For this to work, however, the utility companies must be willing to participate in the net-metering program. Paul Gipe of Real Goods points out that, in contrast to other countries, American utilities pay small-scale wind power producers only 35 to 40 percent of the retail rate, or three or four cents per kilowatt-hour. "This effectively discourages the sale of excess electricity to the utility, even though it is legally permitted," Gipe says. "Under these conditions, the wind turbine must be sized to meet only domestic consumption, limiting home-owners in the United States to small wind turbines."[19]

Several companies are helping to spur the growth of larger scale wind projects. White Wave, the nation's largest

Technologically advanced wind machines like the eggbeater windmill (left) and the vertical axis turbine (right) are extremely efficient.

Large-scale wind farms like this one in Altamont, California, are becoming more practical sources of power as energy-conscious businesses commit to using them.

soy foods manufacturer, has decided to go "green." They are converting all of the energy their company uses to wind energy. The Environmental Protection Agency estimates White Wave's purchase of wind power will keep 32 million pounds of carbon dioxide from being released into the atmosphere. This is the same amount of carbon dioxide released by thirty-five hundred cars being driven for a year. "White Wave has always been committed to socially responsible and environmentally sustainable business practices," says Steve Demos, company founder and president. "This energy ethic is exactly what is needed to bring change in our use of energy." [20]

The U.S. Department of Energy is seeking to have 5 percent of the energy produced in the United States come from wind power by the year 2020. In theory, however, the department says that the world's winds could supply fifteen times the amount of energy currently used worldwide.

Chapter 4

Hydropower

Water, a substance almost as old as the earth itself, covers about three quarters of the planet's surface. It is a very simple molecule, composed of two hydrogen atoms and one oxygen atom, but vital to life on the planet. Water is found in every cell of every plant and animal in the world, and life could not exist without it.

Water moves through the earth's natural systems in what is called the water cycle. The same water molecule may be in a river one day, the sky the next day, on the tip of a glacier the following day, and eventually released back into the atmosphere when the glacier's tip melts. The water molecule itself never changes; it simply changes its location.

As with sunlight, humans have benefited from the energy made available by the presence and movement of water. Waterwheels, turned by the flow of a stream or river pushing against the wooden wheels' paddles, had many uses such as grinding grain into flour, and later, for generating electricity. Dams were also used as early as 1660 in Raj Putana, India, where a marble structure was built to divert water for irrigation and for drinking. Once the principles of electricity became widely known, dams were built to generate electricity. Today, dams are the main tool used to produce hydropower, although water power is still used to turn some waterwheels, grind grain, and pump water. Hydropower produces many benefits, from low-cost electricity to recreational areas, but

Water covers nearly three-fourths of the earth's surface. The movement of water through its natural cycle provides a steady source of energy.

the social and environmental impacts are equally substantial, making this a controversial source of alternative energy.

Harnessing the Water Cycle

That a water molecule changes its location during the water cycle process is quite important to the production of hydropower. Many water molecules that fall onto mountain glaciers or into mountain streams eventually find a path down the mountain and to the ocean. Humans harness the energy of the moving water by constructing dams along the rivers that carry this water. Using the power of water flow to generate electricity is referred to as hydroelectricity.

A dam, also called a hydroelectric power plant, is basically a large concrete structure that blocks the flow of a river. The base of a dam is quite thick and must be set into the bottom of the river. The top of a dam is not as thick and must rise far above the surface of the water. A dam constructed in this manner creates a reservoir of water behind it that looks like a large lake.

To be able to produce electricity, the water from the reservoir must travel through the dam. Power plant operators use a sluice gate, or a controllable opening in the dam, to allow a regulated amount of water to flow through the dam. Because of the pressure from the backed up water in the reservoir, the water entering the sluice gate moves very fast. As the water travels through the dam it flows past turbines which are connected to a generator. Similar to the wind-powered generators, water-powered generators have a large pole inside with metal wires wrapped around it. On the inside walls of

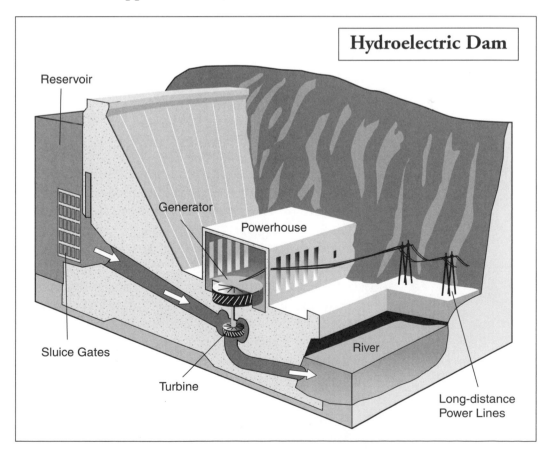

Hydroelectric Dam

Reservoir

Generator

Powerhouse

Sluice Gates

Turbine

River

Long-distance Power Lines

the generator there are magnets and as the turbine poles spin, the magnets also whirl about the metal wires and draw electrons from them. These electrons are sent down other wires as electricity.

The amount of hydroelectricity a dam can produce is related to the amount of water available to send through the dam and the rate at which the water flows. The larger the amount of water in the reservoir and the faster that it flows through the dam, the more electricity the dam can produce.

Hydropower Production

Hydroelectricity accounts for about 10 percent of the electricity produced in the United States. Much of this hydroelectricity is produced at about three hundred different dams, most of which are located in the western United States. The largest of these dams is the Grand Coulee Dam in Washington State. This dam produces about 6,465,000 kilowatts, enough power to continuously satisfy the energy needs of about 250,000 homes.

Other countries in the world rely on hydroelectricity even more than the United States. It is estimated that seven out of ten Canadian homes are powered by hydroelectricity. Hydropower provides Norway with 95 percent of its electrical power and Switzerland with 74 percent. These countries have developed almost every available site on their waterways for producing hydroelectricity.

The largest dam built to date is the Itaipú along the Paraná River in South America. This dam is a joint venture between the countries of Brazil and Paraguay. The sheer amount of building materials and effort that went into the construction of this dam is enormous. The steel and iron used to build this dam would have made 380 Eiffel Towers. According to the American Society of Civil Engineers, the Itaipú Dam workers "reenacted the labor of Hercules; they shifted the course of the seventh largest river in the world and removed more than 50 million tons of earth and rock. The true marvel of Itaipú, though,

is its powerhouse . . . a single building that [continuously] puts out 12,600 megawatts—enough to power most of California."[21]

China is currently constructing a dam even larger than the Itaipú Dam. The Three Gorges Dam on the Yangtze River in China, expected to be completed by 2009, will produce enough electricity to power over 6 million homes, which is about three times that of the South American dam.

The Grand Coulee Dam in Washington is the largest hydroelectric plant in the United States. It produces over 6 million kilowatts of power.

Many Benefits

Hydroelectricity accounts for 80 percent of the renewable energy used in the United States. It is naturally replenished as water travels through the water cycle and provides rivers with water on a continuous basis—both day and night and throughout the seasons. There is never a time when water is not flowing because there is never a full interruption of the water cycle.

Hydroelectricity is also a nonpolluting source of electricity. There are no emissions released by the burning of fuels. The National Hydropower Association estimates that using hydropower instead of burning fossil fuels to create electricity reduces the amount of carbon dioxide released into the atmosphere by about 77 million metric tons. This amount is equivalent to the amount of exhaust from 62.2 million cars being driven for a year, which is about half the cars in the United States.

Hydropower is considered a nonpolluting source of energy for other reasons. Hydropower does not require steam to be released into the atmosphere like several other forms of energy production. Steam can alter weather patterns and requires large quantities of water from the surrounding environment. There are also no chemicals required in the production of hydroelectricity that would have to be disposed of in the environment. Last, since most dams tend to be located in rather remote areas, there is no noise pollution to contend with.

The cost of building a hydroelectric power plant varies widely because each one is built to suit its location. Once such a plant is built, however, the cost to maintain and operate it is fairly minimal in comparison to the income a dam provides the power company. Rarely does a dam need to be shut down for maintenance and even more rarely does a dam break. The life expectancy of any given dam tends to be two to ten times that of a coal or nuclear power plant, which can last up to fifty years. The cost of producing one kilowatt of hydroelectricity is about four cents. This is comparable to the cost of generating power by burning fossil fuels. For many utility companies, the construction of a dam is a wise financial decision in this regard.

The Benefits of Reservoirs

The basic structure of a dam also allows people to benefit beyond the production of electricity. The reservoir, or lake, that builds up behind the dam serves to provide a continual flow of water. It also makes larger amounts of water available to farmers to use downriver during the summer growing season. Under natural conditions, this water would travel from the glaciers on mountaintops to the ocean during the spring runoff, and farmers would have little water to irrigate with. Since the water is reserved for later, it is available for irrigating fields in the spring and early summer.

Many homes in the United States not only receive their electric power from hydroelectric plants but also get their drinking water from the reservoir. For this reason, water treatment plants are often built near a reservoir. The water treatment plants clean the water of harmful bacteria and sediments so that people may use the water in their homes.

The reservoirs behind dams provide recreational opportunities such as boating, water skiing, and fishing. People also like to hike and camp in the natural areas surrounding the reservoirs, or spend time watching the wildlife that is attracted to the water.

Lake Powell was formed with the construction of the Glen Canyon Dam. Such lakes offer recreational activities such as kayaking.

Many hydroelectric dams capitalize on this aspect of their power plants. Duke Power, a company that operates thirty-one hydro projects in North and South Carolina, leases much of the land around their hydroelectric plants to state agencies. These agencies then provide the public with recreational opportunities, such as swimming, boating, hiking, and fishing. In addition, Duke Power has designed and built the Duke Environmental Center, located on the banks of one of their reservoirs, allowing scientists to monitor the overall health of the reservoir waters. The center also serves to educate the public about the benefits of hydropower and its impact on wildlife.

The Social Impacts

Although the water cycle itself is not greatly impacted in the way it is presently being used to produce power, there are many social and ecological impacts. Hydroelectricity requires water to be dammed in a reservoir. The reservoirs behind a dam are often massive. The Glen Canyon Dam, located on the border of Utah and Arizona, virtually drowned the canyon. This meant that all of the people living in that area of about 266 square miles had to be relocated.

It is estimated that when the Three Gorges Dam is completed in China, about 1.9 million people will have to be relocated. This is similar to moving all of the people out of a large city. While some new industries may be created along the Three Gorges Dam, providing employment opportunities for displaced farmers, the transition will be difficult for these people. The end result is that many lives are interrupted and forced in new directions.

After the people are moved from a reservoir site, there are often other social impacts. Historical buildings are sometimes submerged and towns that were once vibrant and bustling become silenced beneath the waters of a reservoir. Reservoir waters can decimate lands and ritual sites that are sacred to Native Americans. For example, in 1942 the Grand Coulee Dam on the Columbia River

took away one of the largest fishing sites in the western United States at Kettle Falls, Washington. Before that time, Native Americans, and later white settlers, came from as far as Oregon, Idaho, Montana, and Canada to participate in the annual salmon harvest at the falls, called by the Native Americans "Shwan-ate-kee," meaning "deep-sounding waters." The harvest provided not only food for the winter but served as a time for social and ceremonial interactions and trading. Once a reservoir is established, there is no going back to re-create the history of the towns and areas hidden beneath its waters.

A group of Chinese displaced by the Three Gorges Dam project disembark from a ferry. By obstructing the flow of the Yangtze, the dam will submerge many towns and villages.

Ecological Impact

When reservoirs are created, they also alter the natural flow of a river. Water that once ran cold and clear down a mountain becomes a large lake that is heated by the sun and often becomes murky from mountain runoff. This ecological change in the water can have unforeseen consequences.

The Aswan Dam in Egypt provides a good example of these consequences. The reservoir there became so warm that a certain kind of parasitic worm began to flourish. Because the reservoir not only served to power many cities in Egypt but was also a source of drinking water, the number of cases of people getting sick and dying from ingesting the parasitic worm went up by about 75 percent. The Aswan Dam is now monitored closely for water temperatures, but people are still wary of drinking from its reservoir.

Another ecological impact of hydroelectricity involves the movement of sediments down the river. Sediments are small particles of soil that are rich in minerals and nutrients. It is made up of decaying plants and animals as well as worn-away bits of rock. The health of animals that live in and along the river depends upon sediment and its minerals.

Usually sediment flows from a mountaintop to the ocean down the course of a river. When a river is dammed, however, the reservoir that is created can act as a large trap for sediment, stopping its downstream progress. Sediment does not go through the dam, and the plants

Fish ladders like this one are built to help fish bypass dams. Fish, however, are often too tired to make the arduous journey along such ladders.

and animals in and along the river downstream from the dam do not get to benefit from the nutrients it provides. At the same time, the animals that live in and along the reservoir get too much of the built-up sediment. It can clog the gills and breathing ways of the aquatic life. The sediment can also slowly poison the animals and plants living in the water. When there is too much sediment in the water, aquatic animals and plants become sick and often die.

The restricted flow of water that a dam imposes also affects wildlife in other ways. Fish, such as salmon, are hatched in riverbeds high in the mountains. These salmon grow into smolts that travel down the river and out to the sea. After several years they return to their original hatch site to spawn and lay their eggs. Dams affect these migrating fish as they head both downstream and upstream.

Young smolts coming down a river to the sea face a huge challenge. Many of these smolts must travel through the internal structures of the dam as they make their journey to the sea. Turbines spin them about and sometimes their bodies are crushed. The Northwest Power Planning Council's Independent Science Group conducted studies in which they established that approximately 15 percent of smolts traveling downstream are killed at each dam. Because many rivers have far more than one dam, these deaths greatly impact salmon populations in the long run.

Fish migrating upstream often find it just as difficult to get past the barriers of a dam. These salmon must navigate the huge distance from the river below a dam to the reservoir waters being held back by the dam. In an effort to solve this problem, many hydroelectric power plant owners install fish ladders, which are a series of cascading pools through which the fish can jump, but these are of little help. Fish are often too tired to face the raging waters and make the sometimes ten- to twenty-foot leaps up the fish ladder. After repeated attempts to climb the fish ladder, many of these salmon perish at the base of a dam. They never make it to their hatch site and never spawn.

The Future of Hydropower

Waterwheels have been used through the ages. The earliest known reference is from around 400 B.C. in the writings of Greek poet Antipater, who wrote of the freedom from toil that the waterwheel provides. From the beginning of modern history the United States has used waterwheels and, later, hydroelectric power plants. Americans understand how hydroelectricity is produced far better than any other renewable resource. They feel comfortable with it, and this comfort goes a long way in helping this renewable resource to flourish.

Currently, only about 2 percent of the rivers in America are free-flowing and not dammed in any manner. This number seems very low and worries many people that Americans are taking advantage of a natural system beyond its capacity to produce. There are many environmental groups seeking to protect these last free rivers. The Wild and Scenic Rivers Act of 1968 protects many of these remaining rivers. It aims to give certain scenic rivers the status of National Parks and protect them from being developed for hydroelectricity.

On the other hand, there are over seventy-five thousand dams along American rivers. Approximately three hundred of them produce substantial amounts of hydroelectricity. The vast majority of the rest of the dams provide irrigation water for farmers; however, many utility companies feel these dams could better serve the energy needs of America if they were accessed for producing hydroelectricity.

Still other groups believe the best sites for generating power from water have already been established. This leaves the country with two options. The first option is for hydroelectric plants to find better ways to maximize the power available at current sites. At present, the majority of dams have an 85 percent efficiency rate. This means dams have the capacity to extract 85 percent of the energy from the movement of water and turn it into electricity. This is quite a high efficiency rate, much higher than burning fossil fuels, which has only a 15 percent efficiency rate for combustion engines. However, many scientists believe it will be hard to improve upon the design of modern dams.

The other option is to start importing more hydroelectricity from neighboring countries such as Canada, which is considered an excellent candidate for such a solution. Canada is rich in fast-flowing rivers with many potential hydroelectric sites that have not yet been developed. Its population is much smaller than the United States' and so it has lower energy needs. As a nation, it already relies heavily on hydroelectricity and has many well-established hydroelectric plants. For these reasons, Canada is being carefully considered as a possible source of electricity to satisfy the energy needs of the American market.

Worldwide, the growth of hydroelectricity is impressive. Already, 20 percent of the electricity produced in the world comes from hydroelectricity. As developing countries seek to bring more power to their countries, they are looking at their major rivers to determine if they can possibly develop sites for hydroelectricity. Laos is currently in the process of developing a 680-megawatt dam that would satisfy the energy needs of most of their citizens. It would also allow for greater economic development within the country as electrical energy is brought to local businesses. With projects such as this in development, it is felt hydroelectricity will become the most established form of renewable energy throughout the world in the decades to come.

Chapter 5

Geothermal Power

S cientists theorize that 15 billion years ago, when the universe was first forming, all matter exploded and released huge amounts of energy. It is this energy that still fuels the sun. It also produces the heat energy found inside the earth, which can be harnessed to create what is called geothermal power.

The earth is in a constant state of change with shifting tectonic plates, erupting volcanoes, and ongoing modification of its internal structures. There are several methods for utilizing geothermal power being explored and developed, but the changing nature of the energy source complicates the process. New technologies are being developed to address these issues, however, which gives new promise for geothermal power as a viable energy source.

Where Geothermal Energy Comes From

When the earth was first forming, about 5 billion years ago, an immense amount of energy was released. Some of this energy was used to bond molecules together very tightly at the center of the earth. These molecules are made mostly of iron and nickel, and they form the inner core of the earth, which is estimated to be about 755 miles in diameter. The earth's inner core, which is relatively cold and solid, is surrounded by an outer core. The outer core, which is a liquid made of the same types of molecules, has a thickness of about 1,410 miles.

Surrounding the outer core of the earth is the mantle. The mantle is about 1,790 miles thick and is made mostly of iron and magnesium. Unlike the core, which is part solid, part liquid, the mantle is completely liquid. It has an average temperature of about thirty-three hundred degrees Fahrenheit. This is very hot and can even melt rocks.

When the heat of the earth's mantle forces the mantle to break through the crust, dramatic volcanic eruptions can result.

As geological time went on, the earth's surface began to cool and a thin crust formed over the mantle. This crust is about 2.5 to 37 miles thick and is made of iron, magnesium, and aluminum. The crust covers the earth's surface and makes up all of the land and the ocean floor.

It is the interaction between the mantle of the earth and the earth's crust that makes geothermal power possible. The crust of the earth traps the heat of the mantle beneath it. Sometimes the heat of the mantle becomes so intense that it causes the mantle to break through at the thinnest areas of the crust. These areas are referred to as hot spots. The material in the mantle can escape at hot spots in the form of volcanic lava. When a volcano

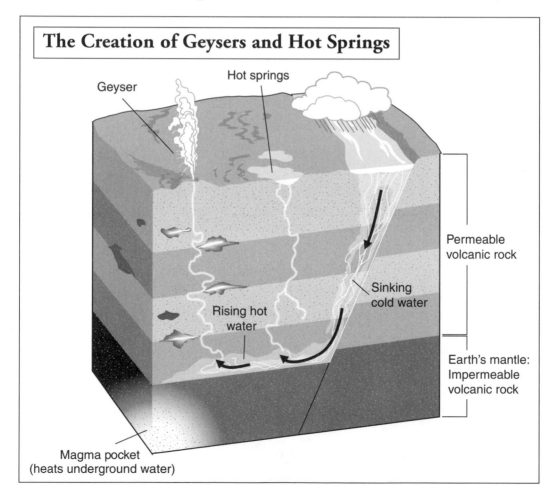

The Creation of Geysers and Hot Springs

Geyser

Hot springs

Permeable volcanic rock

Sinking cold water

Rising hot water

Earth's mantle: Impermeable volcanic rock

Magma pocket (heats underground water)

erupts, it is basically allowing the mantle of the earth to flow up through the crust to the surface.

The heat from the mantle can also come into contact with water in the earth's crust. Underground water sometimes forms large pools and rivers in the crust. When this water comes in contact with the heat of the mantle, it becomes superheated and travels through cracks in the crust to the surface. In this heated state, the water exerts great pressure on the surrounding rocks. The rocks then crack and allow the water to move. The boiling hot water then pushes up through the crust and shoots into the air. This type of geological feature is called a geyser. Yellowstone National Park has many of these geysers, the most famous of which is Old Faithful.

Vents, or cracks and openings, in the earth's crust allow water in the crust to be continuously heated by the mantle. These vents are responsible for such geothermal features as hot springs and geothermal wells full of heated water. The water does not break though the crust and shoot into the air, but is slowly leaked out in the form of steam. These types of hot spots can be found on almost every continent in the world.

Harnessing Geothermal Energy

The heat energy transferred from the mantle to the waters in the earth's crust can be harnessed to create electricity. This can happen in three different ways. Dry steam reservoirs harness the energy of geysers to produce electricity. Wet steam reservoirs use recycled water to make steam deep in the geothermal wells that are heated by the mantle of the earth. Hot water reservoirs create a supply of heated water from underground sources that can be used to heat homes and businesses.

Dry Steam Reservoirs

Dry steam reservoirs use the water in the earth's crust, which is heated by the mantle and released through vents in the form of steam. Dry steam reservoir geothermal plants have pipes that are drilled into the site and used to trap the steam. The steam is then used to turn turbines connected to a generator to produce electricity. This is a highly efficient system for making electricity and has been used by humans for many decades. A large dry steam reservoir near Larderello, Italy, has powered local electric railroads for about one hundred years.

The underground water reservoirs that feed such a system are refilled when rain falls on the land. The rainwater eventually soaks back into the crust of the earth. Because this occurs on a continuous basis, geothermal energy is considered a renewable resource.

About 6 percent of the energy used in northern California is produced at twenty-eight dry steam reservoir plants found at The Geysers dry steam fields in northern California. At peak production, these geothermal power plants can produce up to two thousand megawatts of electricity an hour. That is about twice the amount of electricity a large nuclear power plant can produce.

Wet Steam Reservoirs

Sometimes, however, dry steam reservoirs do not refill themselves in a very consistent manner. They can also have a lower temperature, which results in a less effective combination of water droplets and steam mixed together. Geothermal operators have found a solution to these problems by building wet steam reservoirs. For a wet steam reservoir to work, a well is drilled into the geothermal site to release the steam, which can be anywhere from six hundred to fifteen hundred feet deep. After the steam that is piped up passes through and turns the turbines in the power plant on the surface, it is sent into a condenser, which cools it. This cooled water can then be pumped back into the wells. The water is heated again by the mantle and released as steam. The steam turns the turbines again and produces more electricity. This process can happen over and over with a minimal loss of water. Although there are no current counts of the number of wet steam reservoir plants there are in

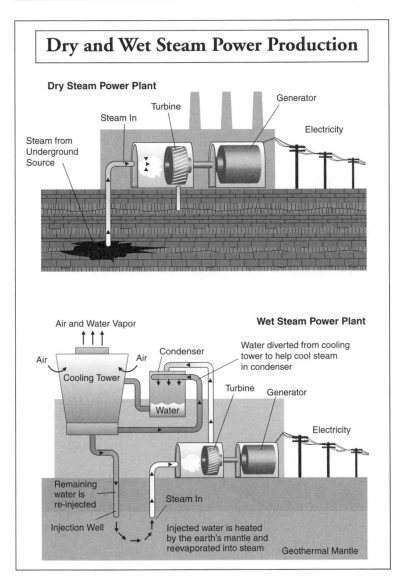

Dry and Wet Steam Power Production

Dry Steam Power Plant

Turbine

Generator

Steam In

Electricity

Steam from
Underground
Source

Wet Steam Power Plant

Air and Water Vapor

Water diverted from cooling
tower to help cool steam
in condenser

Air   Air   Condenser

Cooling Tower

Turbine   Generator

Water

Electricity

Remaining
water is
re-injected

Steam In

Injection Well

Injected water is heated
by the earth's mantle and
reevaporated into steam

Geothermal Mantle

the world, the largest are in New Zealand, Mexico, Japan, and the former Soviet Union.

Hot Water Reservoirs

Geothermal plants built over hot water reservoirs are more common than either dry steam or wet steam reservoir plants. Although the water in a hot water reservoir does not reach high enough temperatures to become steam, it is still valuable. The water itself does not produce electricity, but instead is piped through a network of pipes into the walls of nearby homes and businesses. The heat from the pipes radiates into the rooms, heating the air. Pipes return the water to the hot water reservoir to be reheated and introduced back into the system.

Reykjavik, Iceland, is surrounded by hot water reservoir sites and is also home to about eighty-five thousand people. Almost 80 percent of the homes in this town are heated using hot water reservoir water. There are about 180 locations in the United States that use hot water reservoirs to heat homes, as well as places such as the Utah State Prison in Bluffdale, which is heated solely by geothermal power. These sites could be expanded with further development and by connecting them to the utility company grids. The U.S. Department of Energy believes that developing these sites could produce thirty times more energy than the total amount of energy the country is currently using.

This geothermal plant in Iceland sits atop a hot water reservoir. It supplies the capital city of Reykjavik with heated water.

The Benefits of Geothermal Power

Using the water at geothermal power production sites, whether in the form of steam or hot water, does not deplete the water supply from the surrounding ecosystems as long as it is pumped back into the earth's crust. Because geothermal plants rely upon the interaction of water and molten rocks beneath the crust of the earth, they are also not dependent upon the weather or time of day to produce energy. In addition, the temperatures underground stay consistent throughout the year. For example, a wet water reservoir that has an internal temperature of nearly two thousand degrees Fahrenheit in the summer has the same temperature in the winter. This means geothermal power is available for use twenty-four hours a day, every day of the year. Unlike solar and wind power, the need for battery storage is eliminated because the energy needed to create electricity is always available. This is an attractive feature of any renewable resource.

While geothermal plants need additional replenishing of water supplies because the steam released exceeds the amount of water that naturally flows into the systems, some of these sites are starting to recycle wastewater through their systems as an alternative source of water. Wastewater is all of the water that leaves a home from the sinks, toilets, and outdoor hoses. Some cities are piping their wastewater to geothermal plants. These plants use the wastewater to refill their geothermal wells. The power plants are able to use this steam to create electricity just as if the water had naturally been in the crust of the earth. For example, the city of Santa Rosa, California, pipes its wastewater to its geothermal power plant to replenish the wells. The city receives power from the plant and the water is effectively recycled.

The process used by wet steam geothermal plants requires drilling into the earth's crust. As the hole is drilled, plant operators are left with a lot of sludge. If the sludge, which is often rich in zinc and sulfur, is released into the environment, these elements can be harmful. Fortunately for geothermal plant owners, these two elements can be extracted from the sludge and sold on the market. This also helps make the geothermal plants even more profitable.

Geothermal features, such as geysers and hot springs, are found throughout the world. Yet, to be used to produce geothermal power they must be large in size or have many sites located close together. This type of arrangement happens in only very specific areas on the earth. Countries that have these features, such as New Zealand, Iceland, and Indonesia, have a source of security. They do not have to rely upon other countries to supply energy to their cities and towns. This self-sufficiency allows these countries to make decisions based on what is best for them, not what will make other countries give them energy for a low price.

Advances in geothermal power production have made it competitive with more conventional methods of power production. New drilling techniques and technology, such as 3-D seismic technology as well as advanced directional drilling, which allows drillers to be able to hit an underground target the size of a closet over five miles from the drilling rig and thousands of feet down, help to lower geothermal power production costs. Other cost-saving measures, such as more advanced systems to capture steam, and more recycling of water, have also helped to decrease the cost of geothermal power. Currently, it costs about five cents per kilowatt-hour to produce electricity using geothermal energy, which is only slightly more than the cost of producing electricity by burning fossil fuels. As the price of natural gas and coal increases and the cost of geothermal power decreases, geothermal power is becoming more of an attractive alternative.

The Cost to the Environment

Geothermal power is considered a nonpolluting source of energy, but it does have some serious environmental drawbacks. Often, to develop a geothermal site, frag-

ile ecosystems must be disturbed. Roads must be built to the sites, which are usually remote because the land around geothermal vents is usually too unstable for human habitation. Wells must often be dug, which disrupts the natural flow of groundwater. These actions can impact the surrounding habitat if site development is not managed correctly.

The steam used at geothermal plants can also become a source of air pollution if it is released into the atmosphere. Frequently it is heavily laced with salts and sulfur compounds that are leached from the earth's crust. If the steam is simply condensed and released into the natural waterways, the high levels of salts and sulfurs can be toxic to aquatic wildlife. If released into the air, the toxins, in the form of acid rain, can still find their way into surface water systems and kill aquatic animals. Geothermal plant operators often cool and condense the steam produced at their plants and recycle it into their wells for these reasons.

Sources of geothermal energy like these geysers are usually in remote, uninhabited areas.

The sludge that is created by drilling wells for wet steam geothermal plants can also be a source of environmental pollution. This sludge often contains minerals that contaminate water supplies of local residences if it is not properly processed and disposed of. Aquatic wildlife can also be affected if this sludge is put into the water systems. Strict regulations are in place for most geothermal plants so that both steam and sludge are properly disposed of. However, this often increases the cost of producing geothermal power.

Other Drawbacks

Beyond the environmental impacts that geothermal power production has, there are other significant drawbacks. Geothermal power is not available for a large number of nations. Although geothermal vents are found throughout the world, they are only in large enough numbers to make geothermal power viable in few select areas. The United States has several sites in California and Hawaii. New Zealand, Iceland, and the islands of Indonesia are also rich in geothermal sites.

The basic dynamic of geothermal power can cause problems with energy production as well. Thermal vents, geysers, and hot spots tend to be unstable. Water, rock, and heat are in an ongoing state of interaction and movement, making thermal vent areas relatively uninhabitable. This means that most geothermal sites are in remote areas. Utility lines must be built to the geothermal site in order to carry the electricity to urban areas. This is a very expensive endeavor and often holds back utility companies from building geothermal plants.

Most forms of geothermal energy are not truly renewable resources. Dry steam plants can have problems with the steam at their sites finding new vents to travel through over time. If this occurs, the water would no longer be available to produce geysers and the geothermal plants that rely on these geysers would need to relocate. Wet steam reservoirs have to be constantly supplied with water to produce electricity. Hot water reservoirs can run out eventually and no longer supply water to heat homes.

Yet, since there is so much water in the crust of the earth that is heated by the mantle, it is still considered a renewable resource. It is unlikely that there will ever come a time when water is not heated somewhere in the crust of the earth by the mantle. It is simply a matter of moving geothermal plants to these sites.

Many of these drawbacks to geothermal energy are inherent in its use; there is nothing that can be done to prevent them. There is no way a country can create geothermal features on its land if they do not naturally exist. There is also no available way to create water in sites that need constant replenishing.

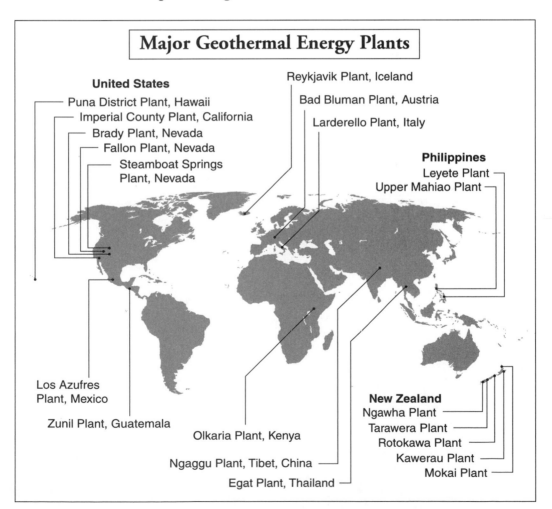

Major Geothermal Energy Plants

United States
Puna District Plant, Hawaii
Imperial County Plant, California
Brady Plant, Nevada
Fallon Plant, Nevada
Steamboat Springs
Plant, Nevada

Reykjavik Plant, Iceland
Bad Bluman Plant, Austria
Larderello Plant, Italy

Philippines
Leyete Plant
Upper Mahiao Plant

Los Azufres
Plant, Mexico

Zunil Plant, Guatemala

Olkaria Plant, Kenya

Ngaggu Plant, Tibet, China

Egat Plant, Thailand

New Zealand
Ngawha Plant
Tarawera Plant
Rotokawa Plant
Kawerau Plant
Mokai Plant

Plumes of steam rise from several sites at this large geothermal plant in Geyserville, California. Because of ongoing improvements in harnessing the earth's internal heat, geothermal energy has a promising future.

Yet, as scientists explore the potential of geothermal power, they are discovering ways to minimize the environmental impact. For example, instead of building more plants, existing sites that were deemed used to capacity and closed are now able to be redrilled using techniques that allow for deeper penetration of the earth's crust. They are also developing systems that allow for steam to be recycled at the site. Perhaps as they progress in their discoveries, many of these challenges to geothermal power will simply become obstacles that were overcome through science.

The Future of Geothermal Power

Currently there are about twenty countries that harness the power of geothermal energy. The United States produces about 45 percent of all geothermal power in the world. Some scientists believe these numbers will increase, as they think the potential for geothermal power has not even begun to be explored. Simply using today's technology and applying it to all available geothermal sites would increase the output of electricity from about 8,240 megawatts to 70,000 megawatts. Using technologies that are being currently researched could increase this figure to as much as 138,000 megawatts. This would be enough power to continuously satisfy about 8 percent of all the energy needs in the world.

A new program called "GeoPowering the West" has been started by the U.S. Department of Energy. This program is designed to give scientists an opportunity to learn more about geothermal energy. Goals of the program include having 7 million homes using geothermal power by 2010, doubling the number of states producing geothermal electricity from four to eight by 2006, and reducing the cost of geothermal power to three cents per kilowatt-hour by 2007. Using the findings from these investigations, the United States will try to meet its goal of using geothermal energy to provide 10 percent of the energy needed by all western states by the year 2020. Kevin Rafferty, associate director for the Geo-Center at Oregon Institute of Technology, is cautious but optimistic about the future of geothermal energy. "Geothermal is unlikely to be the single answer to our energy security any more than wind, solar, conservation, or fossil fuels will be. It should be part of a mix of strategies." In any case, he says, "it can be a much larger part of the energy picture than it is now." [22]

Scientists are also investigating better drilling techniques. It is hoped that they will discover a way to drill into the crust of the earth in the ocean without disturbing the natural cycles of the water. Oceanic crust was selected for these studies because this is where the crust of the earth is the thinnest—sometimes as little as ten miles thick—but still thick enough for drilling. If this investigation is successful, geothermal energy will become an unlimited supply of power for human use. No longer will humans have to rely on natural geothermal features to be able to build geothermal plants. Geothermal power will be able to power human needs for electricity for as long as the mantle of the earth remains hot, which scientists believe will be for hundreds of millions of years more.

Chapter 6

Other Power Alternatives

Solar, wind, hydro, and geothermal power have long been explored by humans as a means for harnessing the energy produced by the natural systems of the earth. Advances in these technologies have started to make each of them a viable alternative to fossil-fuel use. Collectively, these forms of renewable resources account for over 10 percent of the energy produced in the United States. As research and new technology is applied to each one, this percentage is sure to grow.

There are also many other new and intriguing forms of renewable resources that are currently being explored. Some of them are still in the research stages and are not presently making any significant contribution in terms of energy production. Yet they hold immense promise, and energy analysts throughout the world are keeping an eye on their development. Other types of renewable energy sources have gone beyond the research stage and are now being implemented by countries around the world.

OTEC

The ocean is vast. It covers over 75 percent of the earth. The surface waters of the ocean are heated by the energy of the sun. Most of the waters beneath this warm layer remain relatively cold. The abundance of daily sun near the equator creates a significant temperature difference between the warm surface layer of ocean waters and the colder layer below. The vastness of the ocean and the differences in its water temperatures allow it to be used as a renewable source of energy.

An oceanic thermal energy conversion system (OTEC) harnesses the energy of the ocean. An OTEC system is a power plant that is partially submerged in warm, tropical waters. This system relies upon the difference in water temperature between the surface of the ocean and the colder layer below for it to operate. The temperature difference between the surface and the colder layer, which is often about three hundred feet below, can be as much as fifteen to twenty-five degrees Fahrenheit. A tube at the top of the system circulates a liquid such as ammonia, which is heated by the warm surface water on the outside of the tube. The heat changes the ammonia into a gas. This is similar to water being boiled to produce steam. The ammonia gas inside the tube is under a lot of pressure at this point and the pressure turns a turbine generator at the top of the system to produce electricity.

After the ammonia gas pushes past the turbines, it goes into a condenser which uses cold water that is pumped up through a pipe from the bottom layer of the ocean to cool the ammonia inside the tube and return it to a liquid state. The ammonia then runs back into the heating section to repeat the cycle. The design of the system allows the ammonia gas to be used again and again.

An OTEC system is considered a renewable energy source because the temperature differences in the layers of ocean water do not change. The top layer of oceanic water is always warmer and the bottom layers are always colder. The energy is always available to be harnessed by an OTEC system, whether it is used or not.

This type of system is also nonpolluting. Its operation does not require the burning of fossil fuels. It does not produce any chemicals that must be disposed of since all of the chemicals required to operate the system are recycled and remain in the system. OTEC systems are also designed to be located far out in the ocean, causing no noise pollution issues.

A drawback to OTEC systems is the cost of building and operating them. Because all maintenance must be done on-site, a crew must be housed wherever the equipment is located. Crew headquarters and maintenance facilities are built right into the unit's structure, making it much like a small city at sea. The cost of feeding, housing, and paying a crew can offset the profit a utility company may derive from building an OTEC system.

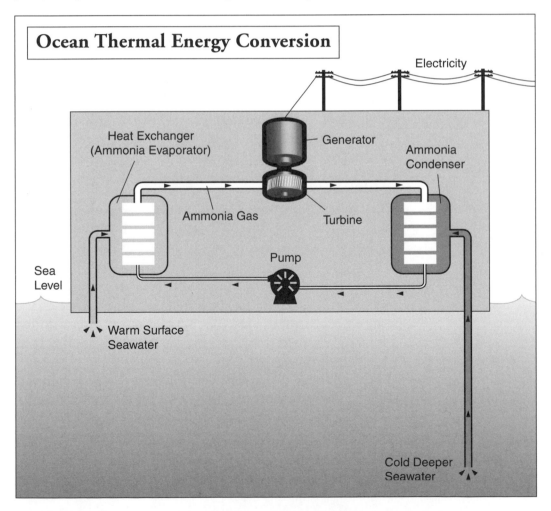

Ocean Thermal Energy Conversion

In theory, an OTEC system could continuously generate upward of 160 million watts of electricity. This amount of electricity could supply one hundred thousand homes with all of their energy needs on a daily basis. Yet, a large portion of this electricity needs to be used by the system itself to pump the cool water to the top of the structure. Many scientists feel this makes an OTEC system a poor choice for energy production.

Presently, the concept of OTEC systems is being heavily researched. Japan has shown great interest in developing them to power its coastal cities. The United States has researched sites where an OTEC system may be effective, but plans to construct one are not yet underway. Some energy analysts believe OTEC systems will never become truly competitive with other renewable resources because of the high cost of building and maintaining the units. This, coupled with a low energy output, in comparison to the amount of energy used to run the system itself, may help to explain why OTEC systems have not yet been fully developed, although the concept has been researched for over fifty years.

Tidal Power

Not only is the ocean vast, it is also powerful. Every day the ocean releases huge amounts of energy in the form of tides. These tides are created by the gravitational pull of the moon on the earth's waters. As ocean tides rise, billions of gallons of water are pushed onto the land. As the ocean tide goes out, billions of gallons of water are carried back into the sea. The movement of this amount of water requires a lot of energy. It is this energy that can be harnessed to create electricity.

There are two main ways that have been developed for the energy of tides to be used to produce electricity. The first way requires a large tidal dam, called a barrage, to be built across an estuary with a high tide range. An estuary is an area where a river runs into the ocean. Often an estuary is located at a bay or inlet. Either is a perfect site for a barrage because it is relatively calm and

although the tide moves in and out, there is no hard, pounding surf.

A barrage is structured like a long cement wall, sometimes over one thousand feet long, with gates in it. The gates are lifted during low tide, which allows water to flow into the estuary as the tide is coming in. When the estuary has filled with water, the gates are lowered and the water can only leave by traveling through turbines in the underwater wall that are connected to generators to produce electricity. La Rance Tidal Power Plant, the largest barrage tidal power station, is located in France. Situated in the estuary of the Rance River as it flows into the English Channel, it is able to produce enough electricity to continuously power fifteen hundred homes.

The second way tides are used to produce electricity requires the building of tidal stream "windmills." These windmill structures are placed in the tidal currents that are along coastlines. The blades of the windmill turn

A dam built across an estuary with a high tidal range can harness the power of the tidal movement to generate electricity.

as water pushes past them. The concept is very similar to the generation of electricity using wind power, but because water is much denser than air, the force of a typical tidal movement on a water windmill would be like that of a hurricane on a wind turbine.

When harnessed by barrages and water windmills, the tides are considered renewable resources. The tides of the ocean are forever occurring because it is the pull of the moon and the rotation of the earth that causes them. As long as the moon exists and the world rotates, tidal power can be harnessed.

Barrages and water windmills are nonpolluting sources of energy. There are no fossil fuels being burned to create power. There are also no chemicals involved in producing the electricity. There is not any wastewater emission or air pollution released into the atmosphere.

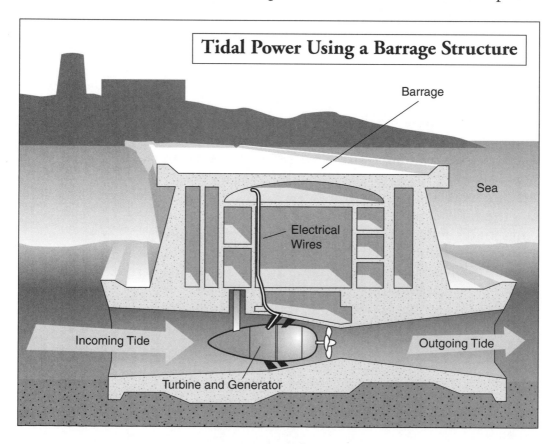

Tidal Power Using a Barrage Structure

Barrage

Sea

Electrical Wires

Incoming Tide

Outgoing Tide

Turbine and Generator

Both barrages and water windmills are considered a green form of energy production.

There are a number of negative aspects to using barrages and water windmills to produce electricity, however. There are few sites in the world that have been developed for this type of power generation, making tidal power one of the world's largest untapped energy reserves. This lack of commitment to the research and development of construction sites is why only France, Canada, and the former Soviet Union are currently producing significant amounts of electricity using tidal power. Both types of tidal power plants are also, at present, very expensive to construct. Ocean waters tend to be corrosive as well and so tidal power plants require ongoing maintenance. All three of these factors make tidal power unattractive to many utility companies.

Due to these challenges, tidal power may never become a major source of electricity for the world, despite its great potential. Yet, this form of energy will be sure to expand to some degree as the fossil fuel reserves continue to be depleted. As new technologies develop, some coastal cities may be able to satisfy a percentage of their energy needs using tidal power.

Biomass

Humans have burned wood as a source of heat for all of recorded history. Wood is a type of biomass, or fuel that comes from burning plant material. There are two different ways to harness the energy released when biomass is burned. Biofuel use can be in the form of direct burning of plant materials, like wood, or using plant materials to produce alcohol that may be burned.

Direct burning of biofuels represents 13 percent of the energy produced in the world. Most of this type of biofuel burning is in the form of wood. Approximately 70 percent of the homes in developing countries use biofuels to heat their homes and to cook food. People in these areas gather firewood as a part of their daily chores and bring it home to be burned. About 20 percent of

American homes burn wood as one of their heat sources, while 5 percent of American homes rely solely on firewood as a source of heat. It is understandable why biofuel, in the form of wood, is considered an important part of the world's energy production.

Plant materials, such as sugarcane, seaweed, and corn husks, may also be burned to produce energy. These plant materials are often what are left over after farmers have processed them. Spain has three biofuel power plants that burn the materials left over from processing olive oils and produce enough electricity to power one hundred thousand homes.

Municipal waste can also be burned as a type of biofuel. Municipal waste is all of the garbage that is generated in a home or business. Many cities in Japan, the United States, and western Europe incinerate their municipal waste to make electricity. The heat from burning the refuse is used to boil water into steam. The steam is used to drive turbines that are connected to generators that create electricity. The United States has 110 of these incineration sites. Each of these sites is able to produce enough electricity to power sixty thousand homes. Biofuel in this form plays an important role in American energy production.

Landfills, where garbage is disposed of, produce biofuel as well. Landfills are designed so that the waste materials delivered each day are covered with soil at the end of the day. Waste that is covered in this manner uses anaerobic bacteria to decompose. Anaerobic bacteria produce methane gas as they decompose the waste. Methane gas is highly flammable and may be burned to boil water into steam to power turbines that generate electricity. This type of biofuel use has an additional benefit. Methane gas is one of the most harmful of the greenhouse gases. Burning methane gas to create electricity helps to reduce the amount of methane gas in the atmosphere. Less methane gas means a reduction in the rate of global warming.

Yeast plays a vital role in the formation of another biofuel: ethanol. Yeast uses a process called fermentation to break down plant materials such as grain. Ethanol, a gas produced by yeast as it digests grain, can be burned to generate the heat needed to create steam used in the production of electricity. The country of Brazil relies heavily on ethanol as a biofuel. Many of Brazil's sugarcane processing plants use yeast to digest the leftover plant materials. The ethanol produced is mixed with gasoline to produce gasohol. Almost one-third of the cars in Brazil operate on gasohol. The United States produced 1.5 billion gallons of ethanol fuel in 1999. This ethanol is used to support electricity production and is also used in some motor vehicles in the form of gasohol.

Using biofuels as a source of energy does have some environmental impacts. Whenever any plant material is burned, carbon dioxide is released into the atmosphere. In developed countries there are some regulations intended to help reduce the amount of carbon dioxide released into the atmosphere from burning biofuels.

Trash is a form of biofuel. Garbage is stored in this large holding area before being burned to create steam to generate electricity.

Another negative aspect of biofuel production is that producing the plant materials needed for biofuels requires a lot of land space. It takes about ten acres of land to produce enough biofuel to match the energy output that one acre of land devoted to solar power production can produce. It is this fact that keeps biofuels from becoming a central focus on the spectrum of renewable energy choices.

Hydrogen

Hydrogen is one of the most abundant elements in the world. It is found everywhere: in the air, the land, and water. Beyond solar power, it is the most unlimited source of energy known to humankind. Unfortunately, it is also proving to be the hardest form of energy to harness.

Hydrogen and oxygen are the two elements that combine to make water. This bond is very strong and it requires a massive input of energy to break apart the hydrogen and oxygen atoms. But once the bond is broken, hydrogen becomes a gas that is highly flammable. Hydrogen gas can be burned to run combustion engines such as those in cars.

The most exciting aspect of hydrogen energy is that when it is burned, it simply recombines with the oxygen in the air to create water. There are no emissions of carbon dioxide or other environmentally damaging gases. Hydrogen power has the potential to be the cleanest form of energy developed by humans.

The process of breaking atoms of hydrogen and oxygen apart, however, requires more energy than can be gained from burning the hydrogen itself. To make hydrogen power a reality, scientists are exploring ways to break apart the water molecules using sources of energy that are abundant and do not damage the environment. They are looking to solar and wind power for outside power. If they are successful, many energy analysts believe hydrogen power will replace fossil fuels as the number one source of energy in the world within the next fifty years.

Scientists have to address more than just the issue of having the energy for separating hydrogen and oxygen if they are to bring hydrogen to the world market. Because hydrogen is a gas, it takes up quite a lot of space, a lot more than gasoline (gasoline is truly a liquid and is only turned into combustible gas vapors by the heat of an engine). Automobiles would have to be designed to carry a large volume of hydrogen gas. The amount of space required means these automobiles would not have a very fuel-efficient design. The energy benefit of using hydrogen would be lost in having to carry the extra weight of a large hydrogen gas tank.

But some researchers have found a solution to this problem. They have redesigned car engines so that instead of burning the hydrogen, it is recombined with oxygen to produce electricity, which the cars use in place of fossil fuels. Automobiles powered in this manner are said to be powered by fuel cells. Vehicles powered by fuel cells are quiet, efficient, and nonpolluting when the hydrogen gas is produced using solar power.

A Ford Motor Company executive demonstrates a hydrogen-fueled electric car. Hydrogen fuel cells are a promising energy alternative.

Hydrogen is also safer than gasoline because it is completely nontoxic, impossible to contaminate, and if leaked, tends to disperse upward because it is so light. Unlike a gasoline-powered vehicle, there are no moving parts, such as a combustion engine, needed to convert hydrogen to electricity, and so the engine will not wear out.

Fuel cells are difficult to acquire, although the fuel cell market for transportation is growing. The federal government has partnered with several automobile manufacturers to develop concept cars that are highly efficient. This merging of interests, called the Partnership for a New Generation of Vehicles, has, so far, found success. The first of these concept cars was revealed at the North American International Auto Show in January 2000. This car is able to accelerate from zero to sixty miles an hour

A strong commitment of money and research is needed if alternative energy facilities like this tidal generating station are to become viable power producers.

in nine seconds and is able to get the energy equivalent of 108 miles to the gallon. Many people in the automobile industry are excited about the development of cars that use fuel cell power and are looking into designing their own models.

Currently, however, cars powered solely on fuel cell energy are still in the development stage. There will have to be many changes in the infrastructure of American gas stations before cars powered by fuel cells can be successfully brought to the open market. Hydrogen will have to be provided as readily as gasoline before the average American consumer is able to buy a fuel cell–powered car. A market for the cars will have to be developed to make production profitable. Once these challenges are overcome, there may be many Americans who will one day be driving cars powered by fuel cells.

The Future for Other Power Alternatives

OTEC, tidal power, biomass, and hydrogen power may all seem unlikely sources of energy, but the technology is already available. None of these forms of power has yet been perfected. Each one has its own set of challenges in development. Each has its own drawbacks. There will need to be a commitment of money, research, and time devoted to furthering these alternative energy sources before they are available as viable energy options for the average consumer.

Yet, each one holds promise for the future. These forms of energy are completely renewable. They do not release harmful pollutants into the environment. Any one of these renewable resources may hold the key to a sustainable future. Together they may each play a small role in making the world a cleaner and healthier place to live for generations to come.

Epilogue

Looking Toward a Sustainable Future

The largest impact that will be made in the world of energy production will most likely come from government policies. However much progress is made toward the production of efficient, inexpensive, renewable energy, it can never be fully implemented on a nationwide level without the backing and support of the U.S. government. There are many steps the government can take to help growth of renewable energy sources, making the United States less dependent on fossil fuels and opening the door to a sustainable energy future.

Government Support

The U.S. government can provide financial support for the exploration of renewable energy sources. This support can be in the form of grants given to researchers so they may experiment with renewable energy technology. The Department of Energy has developed a grant-based research project called the Climate Change Technology Initiative (CCTI). The CCTI seeks to find ways to reduce the emission of greenhouse gases. As part of·this research project, the CCTI helps fund the Partnership for a New Generation of Vehicles. The partnership was formed between major car manufacturers and the U.S. government with the hope that technology developed through this research will reduce the amount of carbon dioxide emitted from cars in the United States. The grant also supports other experiments on new renewable energy resources.

To help advance renewable energy sources, the government can also support consumers who choose renewable energy sources over more traditional energy sources. Consumers can be given tax credits for purchasing solar panels, wind machines, or clean-fuel-burning cars. These tax credits would offset the high initial cost of these energy sources and make purchasing them more attractive to many people. Citizens of the state of Iowa have such a tax credit mandated in their state. Any materials purchased to produce either solar or wind power is exempt from state sales tax.

The U.S. government also can exercise its authority to order public utility companies to purchase excess power created by renewable energy resources, called net

In 1999 President Clinton signs an executive order creating an agency to research the potential of renewable energy sources.

metering. The resources involved in net metering must meet two requirements to be purchased: The site of production must be on the grid of the utility company, and the electricity being generated must be compatible with the utility company's system. If these two conditions are met, the government can enforce regulations that require excess energy produced at these sites to be purchased by the utility companies. Many of the public utility companies in California are currently purchasing green energy from renewable energy sites. This arrangement is considered a win-win situation for both renewable energy production plants and overburdened public utility companies. Pacificorp is one Northwest utility company that has recently opened itself to net metering. Sonja Ling of the Renewable Northwest Project, which helped petition Pacificorp to adopt a net metering policy, says "Net-metering for small-scale, clean, renewable energy systems is one important step towards diversifying the region's energy mix and reducing our overdependence on hydropower and fossil fuels." [23]

As in the cases of Iowa's tax incentives and California's buyback of excess power, actions of support for renewable energy by the U.S. government are generally accepted by most businesses and consumers. Such steps are seen as having the potential to go a long way in supporting renewable resources if they are implemented and followed through on in the years to come. As the government implements these measures, analysts claim that renewable resources will see steady growth.

The Influence of Big Oil Companies

There are other measures that support the growth of renewable resources that the government has the option to take. These measures, not generally favored by some large businesses and some consumers, tend to be the most controversial. They are also seen as the actions that will help to ensure the quickest and most thorough transition from fossil fuels to renewable resources. For example, renewable energy proponents say the gov-

ernment can stop leasing public lands at extremely low prices to companies that drill and mine for fossil fuels. In this case consumers, as well as the oil companies, say they do not want to see a price increase on these lands because it would result in higher prices for the oil companies' products.

Energy analysts say that currently the U.S. government spends many times more the amount of money researching the efficiency of fossil fuels than it does the possibilities of renewable resources. This money could be shifted into programs that support the growth of renewable energy instead. In a study conducted by Research/Strategy/Management Inc. of Sterling, Virginia,

Greenpeace activists fly a hot-air balloon over Park City, Utah, with a message stressing the need to shift to clean and renewable energy sources.

37 percent of American consumers said renewable energy should receive the most in research funding, while only 8 percent said research concerning fossil fuel should be of the highest priority. The other 55 percent said they felt funding should be spent in other areas. In this case, the oil industry and consumers seem to be in opposition concerning the proper focus for government-funded energy research.

The U.S. government has the power to greatly influence the development of renewable resources in this nation. Many energy analysts believe there will be no significant growth in renewable energy resources unless the government uses that power. Critics say that the legislation the government passes concerning energy production is often influenced greatly by large oil companies whose profits depend on producing fossil fuels. Some voters support such legislation because they simply want cheap gas. Others want an alternative source of power that will leave their children with a clean planet. Many people feel the decision to move toward a sustainable energy future requires that voters and corporations alike accept the responsibility of being stewards of the land instead of thinking only about financial gains.

Notes

Chapter 1: The Development of Energy

1. Laughton Johnston, *Climate Change and Scotland: After the Flood.* Triple Echo, 2003, p. 14.
2. Ralph Nansen, *Sun Power: The Global Solution for the Coming Energy Crisis.* Ocean Shores, WA: Ocean Press, 1995, p. 3.
3. Johnston, *Climate Change and Scotland,* p. 15.
4. Quoted in *Arizona Business Gazette,* "Renewable Energy," August 14, 2003. www.azcentral.com/abgnews/articles/0814RENEW 14.html.
5. Melvin A. Benarde, *Our Precarious Habitat.* New York: W.W. Norton, 1970, p. 323.
6. John J. Berger, *Charging Ahead.* New York: Henry Holt, 1997, p. 3.
7. Steve Kretzmann, Foreword, in , Jennifer Carless, *Renewable Energy: A Concise Guide to Green Alternatives.* New York: Walker, 1993, p. vii.
8. Berger, *Charging Ahead,* pp. 3–4.
9. Laurie Burnham, ed., *Renewable Energy: Sources for Fuels and Electricity.* Washington, DC: Island Press, 1993, p. 1.

Chapter 2: Solar Power

10. Carless, *Renewable Energy: A Concise Guide to Green Alternatives,* p. 34.
11. John Schaeffer, *Solar Living Source Book.* White River Junction, VT: Chelsea Green, 2002, p. 61.
12. Carless, *Renewable Energy: A Concise Guide to Green Alternatives,* p. 26.
13. Richard Golob and Eric Brus, *The Almanac of Renewable Energy.* New York: Henry Holt, 1993, p. 125.
14. Golob and Brus, *The Almanac of Renewable Energy,* p. 125.
15. Carless, *Renewable Energy: A Concise Guide to Green Alternatives,* p. 34.

Chapter 3: Wind Power

16. Quoted in *Northwest Science & Technology,* "How Will We Power Our Future?" Autumn 2002, p. 19.

17. Quoted in *Wind Energy Weekly,* "Construction Begins on First Phase of 250-MS Wind Project," March 1, 1999. www.awea. org/wew/837-2.htm.

18. Quoted in Renewable Northwest Project, "New Net-Metering Standard Benefits Pacificorp Customers, Region's Economy and the Environment," June 23, 2003. www.rnp.orgh/News/ pr_IDNETMETERJUNE03.html.

19. Quoted in Schaeffer, *Solar Living Source Book,* p. 140.

20. Quoted in White Wave, "White Wave Invests in Wind to Fuel Soy Manufacturing," February 3, 2003. www.whitewave.com/ index.php?id=108&pid=27.

Chapter 4: Hydropower

21. Quoted in Modern Wonders, "Modern Wonders: Itaipú Dam," January 16, 2000. www.ce.eng.usf.edu/pharoos/wonders/ Modern/itaipu.html.

Chapter 5: Geothermal Power

22. Quoted in *Northwest Science & Technology,* "How Will We Power Our Future?" p. 22.

Epilogue: Looking Toward a Sustainable Future

23. Renewable Northwest Project, "New Net-Metering Standard Benefits Pacificorp Customers, Region's Economy and the Environment."

For Further Reading

Books

Donna Bailey, *Energy from Wind and Water.* Austin, TX: Steck-Vaughn, 1991. Examines various methods for harnessing energy from wind and water. Explores the history of both wind and water as power sources.

Bob Brooke, *Solar Energy.* New York: Chelsea House, 1992. Discusses the pros and cons of solar energy. Explains the history of solar power use and takes a look at new solar energy technology.

Gary Chandler and Kevin Graham, *Alternative Energy Sources.* New York: Twenty-first Century, 1996. Explores various alternative energy projects currently being developed. Interviews key people regarding their roles in the project.

Ewan McLeish, *Energy Resources: Our Impact on the Planet.* Orlando, FL: Raintree Steck-Vaughn, 2002. An informative book about the impact human activities are having on our environment.

Christine Petersen, *Alternative Energy.* Chicago: Childrens, 2004. A complete look at all the major forms of alternative energy and their current uses.

Graham Rickard, *Water Energy.* Milwaukee, WI: Gareth Stevens, 1991. Describes the history of water energy and current methods of harnessing hydropower using dams.

Robert Snedden, *Energy Alternatives.* Oxford, England: Heinemann Library, 2001. An exploration of renewable energy sources on a global level.

Margaret Spence, *Solar Power.* New York: Gloucester, 1993. Describes how the energy of the sun can be harnessed by both passive and active solar systems and how to apply these systems in the home.

Web Sites

EIA Kids' Page, Department of Energy (www.eia.doe.gov/kids). An interactive Web site for children to learn facts about alternative energy through a series of games and quizzes.

Foundation for Water and Energy Education (www.fwee.org). Learners are offered facts about hydroelectricity and can take a virtual tour of a hydropower plant.

Los Angeles Unified School District (www.lausd.net). The official site of the Los Angeles Unified School District, which includes a student-generated Web site that explores various alternative fuel systems for cars.

Roofus' Solar and Efficient Neighborhood, U.S. Department of Energy (www.eere.energy.gov/roofus). An interactive Web site that uses an animated dog to guide learners through a home while pointing out various energy conservation techniques.

Works Consulted

Books

Melvin A. Benarde, *Our Precarious Habitat*. New York: W.W. Norton, 1970. Proposes the need to adequately explore the impact human activities have on the environment in relation to food production, energy consumption, and pollution issues before implementing large-scale changes.

John J. Berger, *Charging Ahead*. New York: Henry Holt, 1997. An investigation into the ways in which small businesses and organizations are using renewable energy sources as viable alternatives to burning fossil fuels.

Godfrey Boyle, ed., *Renewable Energy: Power for a Sustainable Future*. New York: Oxford University Press, 1996. Provides strong descriptions of the chief alternative sources, including the physical principle driving the energy source and the impact they may have on the environment.

Laurie Burnham, ed., *Renewable Energy: Sources for Fuels and Electricity*. Washington, DC: Island Press, 1993. An assessment of the overall performance, cost, market potential, and environmental impact for all major sources of alternative energy.

Jennifer Carless, *Renewable Energy: A Concise Guide to Green Alternative*. New York: Walker, 1993. Presents the current status of renewable resources used in the United States, along with the future outlook of these resources and the impact they have on the environment.

Nancy Cole and P.J. Skerrett, *Renewables Are Ready: People Creating Renewable Energy Solutions*. New York: Chelsea Green, 1995. A guide for communities interested in bringing alternative energy sources to their areas. Showcases a number of successful community endeavors in alternative energy use.

James T. Dulley, *Earth Friendly Home: Alternative Energy for Your Home*. Cincinnati, OH: WWW Books, 1999. Comprehensive overview of the principal renewable energy sources.

Rex A. Ewing and LaVonne Ewing, *Logs, Wind and Sun: Handcraft Your Own Log Home . . . Then Power It with Nature*. Masonville, CO: RixyJack, 2002. An information-packed book about building a log home and using alternative power production methods such as wind and solar power.

Diane Gibson, *Hydroelectricity*. North Mankato, MN: Smart Apple Media, 2002. Discusses the benefits and drawbacks of hydroelectricity and examines the process of producing electricity from hydropower.

———, *Solar Power*. North Mankato, MN: Smart Apple Media, 2002. Explores the history of solar power, how it works, and the pros and cons of its use.

Paul Gipe, *Wind Power for Home and Business*. White River Junction, VT: Chelsea Green, 1993. An intermediate book that offers pros and cons of wind power use for the typical consumer.

Richard Golob and Eric Brus, *The Almanac of Renewable Energy*. New York: Henry Holt, 1993. A guide to the history and use of renewable energy and a prediction of future renewable energy uses.

Martin Green, *Power to the People: Sunlight to Electricity Using Solar Cells*. Sydney, Australia: New South Wales University Press, 2000. Explores the connection between fossil-fuel use and global warming. The author makes a strong case for the use of solar power.

Laughton Johnston, *Climate Change and Scotland: After the Flood*. Triple Echo, 2003. Accompanies BBC Radio Scotland's environmental series *Fresh Air,* broadcast between February 19 and March 26, 2003.

Dermot McGuigan, *Harnessing the Wind for Home Energy*. Charlotte, VT: Garden Way, 1978. A beginners' guide to harnessing wind power while providing readers with geographical information about areas best suited for wind power.

Ralph Nansen, *Sun Power: The Global Solution for the Coming Energy Crisis*. Ocean Shores, WA: Ocean Press, 1995. Explores the implementation of a solar power program in regard to its application to outer space.

Mukund R. Patel, *Wind and Solar Power Systems*. Boca Raton, FL: CRC, 1999. Comprehensive study of the wind and solar power systems, covering the design and operation of each.

Dan Ramey, *The Complete Idiot's Guide to Solar Power for Your Home*. Indianapolis, IN: Alpha, 2003. A beginners' resource manual that describes the techniques required to bring solar power into the home.

John Schaeffer, *Solar Living Source Book*. White River Junction, VT: Chelsea Green, 2002. A descriptive catalog of renewable energy products providing consumer information about current renewable energy use in the United States.

Ralph Wolfe and Peter Clegg, *Home Energy for the Eighties*. Charlotte, VT: Garden Way, 1979. Explores all major sources of alternative energy as they apply to home energy needs. Stresses the importance of moving away from fossil fuels.

Periodical

Northwest Science & Technology, "How Will We Power Our Future?" Autumn 2002.

Internet Sources

Arizona Business Gazette, "Renewable Energy," August 14, 2003. www.azcentral.com/abgnews/articles/0814RENEW14.html.

The Digital Collegian, "U.S. Biotechnology Grant to Help Renewable Energy Research," September 16, 2003. www.collegian.psu.edu/archive/2003/09-16-03dnews-03.asp.

Modern Wonders, "Modern Wonders: Itaipú Dam," January 16, 2000. www.ce.eng.usf.edu/pharoos/wonders/Modern/itaipu.html.

Renewable Northwest Project, "New Net-Metering Standard Benefits Pacificorp Customers, Region's Economy and the Environment," June 23, 2003. www.rnp.orgh/News/pr_IDNETMETERJUNE03.html.

White Wave, "White Wave Invests in Wind to Fuel Soy Manufacturing," February 3, 2003. www.whitewave.com/index.php?id=108&pid=27.

Wind Energy Weekly, "Construction Begins on First Phase of 250-MS Wind Project," March 1, 1999. www.awea.org/wew/837-2.htm.

Web Sites

American Wind Energy Association (www.awea.org/wew/837-2.html). Provides an overview of the use of wind energy and its current production levels in the United States as well as links to other wind energy sites.

Arizona Business Gazette (www.azcentral.com). A business journal catering to the needs of Arizona-based businesses and exploring the issues impacting them, including developments in energy alternatives in the state of Arizona.

Back Woods Solar (www.backwoodssolar.com). Back Woods Solar Electric Systems specializes in solar-generated electricity for remote homes where utility lines are not available or not practical to access.

By Design (www.bydesign.com/fossilfuels/links/index.html). One thousand annotated links for learning how North America uses fossil fuels.

Climate Solutions (www.climatesolutions.org). Climate Solutions sponsors a variety of programs to help stop global warming.

The Digital Collegian (www.collegian.psu.edu). An Internet-based publication created by students at Penn State that includes thought-provoking articles on a variety of topics, such as energy alternatives.

Elsevier (www.elsevier.com). A world-leading publisher of scientific, technical, and health information, such as the *Journal of Environmental Psychology,* and other environmental publications that include discussions of energy alternatives.

Energy Central (www.energycentral.com). Provides up-to-date information about the global power industry.

Energy Quest (www.energyquest.ca.gov/index.html). Energy Quest is the award-winning energy education Web site of the California Energy Commission. Site creators believe energy is an "integral part of our daily lives" and that today's youth must be relied upon to "create new ways to harness the elemental forces of our planet and the universe."

Home Power (www.homepower.com). Provides information on how to use solar, hydroelectric, or wind energy to provide a home or business with electricity.

JATS Alternative Power Company (www.jatsgreenpower.com). Alternative energy provider supplying solar, wind, and mini-hydropower equipment for producing electricity and heating, using renewable energy.

National Renewable Research Laboratory (www.nrel.gov/otec/what.html). Provides information about ocean thermal energy conversion (OTEC), an energy technology that uses the temperature differences in the ocean to produce power.

Renewable Energy Atlas (www.energyatlas.org). An eighty-page, full-color, printable online presentation of the renewable energy resources in the western United States, including newly released high-resolution wind maps of the Pacific Northwest. The Atlas profiles wind, solar, geothermal, and biomass power.

Renewable Northwest Project (www.rnp.org). In 1994 a broad coalition of public-interest organizations and energy companies created the Renewable Northwest Project (RNP) to actively promote development of the region's untapped renewable resources.

Solarbuzz (www.solarbuzz.com). Provides current news of the solar power industry and a "helicopter view" of where the solar photovoltaic (PV) industry stands using industry statistics.

Southwest Windpower (www.windenergy.com). Site described as "The World Leader in Micro-Windenergy," providing wind energy information in a user-friendly format.

University of Washington Center for Urban Horticulture (www.cfr.washington.edu/research.envmind). Features research on perceptions and behaviors of people regarding nature in cities.

U.S. Department of Energy, Energy Efficiency and Renewable Energy (www.eere.energy.gov/state_energy/index.cfm). A gateway to hundreds of Web sites and thousands of online documents on energy efficiency and renewable energy.

White Wave (www.whitewave.com). A soy products manufacturing company dedicated to being a leader in the world of environmentally conscious businesses.

World Energy (www.worldenergy.net). The nation's largest provider of alternative fuel solutions for federal, state, utility, transit, municipal, and private fleets nationwide.

Index

Picture Credits

About the Author

Gabriel Cruden is a journalist, photographer, and environmental educator who lives in rural northeast Washington State. He lives off the grid in a straw-bale house he helped to build in the early 1990s. He believes that through communication, education, and appreciation of the natural world, humanity can successfully learn to live lightly on the land.

112